Using Offshore Trusts, Annuities, and Portfolio Bonds

Using Offshore Trusts, Annuities, and Portfolio Bonds

Ingenious Ways to Preserve Your Wealth

Edited by
Martin Schuster

Books for Business
New York - Hong Kong

Using Offshore Trusts, Annuities, and
Portfolio Bonds:
Ingenious Ways to Preserve Your Wealth

Edited by
Martin Schuster

ISBN: 0-89499-202-3

Copyright © 2002 by Books for Business

Books for Business
New York - Hong Kong
http://www.BusinessBooksInternational.com

Offshore Trusts
Copyright © by Adam Starchild

Asset Protection Through Swiss Life Insurance Policies
Copyright © by Marc Sola

Investing Offshore Through Portfolio Bonds
Copyright © by Marc Sola

All rights reserved, including the right to reproduce this book, or portions thereof, in any form.

Offshore Trusts

Adam Starchild

Asset Protection Through Swiss Life Insurance Policies

Marc Sola

Investing Offshore Through Portfolio Bonds

Marc Sola

Offshore Trusts

by Adam Starchild

Introduction: "Trust Me" -- A Word About Trusts 6

A Short History of Trusts 8
    An Ancient Custom 8
    The First Roman Trust 9
    European Trust Law 10
    English and American Origins 11
    Trust Evolution 13
    Charitable Gifts and the Civil Law 14
    Modern Uses 15
    Social and Economic Uses 17
    Commercial Functions 17
    Estate Planning 18
    Asset Protection 19

Trust Purposes and Principles 20
    Anatomy of a Trust 20
    Decisions and a "Declaration" 21
    Judicial Definitions 23
    What A Trust Is Not 24
    Trust Location 25
    Change of Trust "Situs" 26
    Choosing a Trust Situs 27
        General Reasons 27
        Tax Reasons 27
    Basics of Trust Creation 28
    The Corpus 29
    The Living Trust 31
    Advantages and Disadvantages 32
    Trusts: Revocable and Irrevocable 33
    The Revocable Living Trust 34

Lack of Asset Protection 36
Sure Asset Protection 36
Irrevocable Living Trusts 37
Comparative Tax Advantages for American Settlors 39
The Testamentary Trust 41
Express and Implied 42
It Takes Getting Used To 43

Parties, People, Powers 44
The Settlor 44
Settlor/Trustee as Beneficiary 45
Choosing a Trustee 47
  An Individual Trustee 47
  A Corporate Trustee 48
Co-Trustees 48
Duties of a Trustee 49
Trustee Powers, Express and Implied 52
The "Prudent Investor" Rule 53
Trust Investor Rule Update 55
Guidelines for Trustee Investments 56
Support for the Beneficiary 57
Frequency of Trust Payments 57
Care, Support and Maintenance 58
Beneficiary Rights and Duties 60
Beneficiary Liabilities 61
Limited Beneficiary Rights 62
Duration of a Trust 63

Trusts for Business and Investment 65
The Business Trust 65
  Trusts and Family Businesses 66
Investment Trusts 67
  Real Estate Investment Trusts (REITs): 68
  Royalty investment trusts: 69
  Unit investment trusts: 69
  Miscellaneous investment trusts: 69

The Offshore Asset Protection Trust 71
    Up Front Costs 72
    Where To Establish an APT 73
    Strong Creditor Deterrent 74
    Creating an APT 76
    Operating a Foreign APT 77
    APT Combined With a Limited Partnership 78
    U.S. Tax Consequences for our American Readers 79
    Avoiding Income Tax on APT Income 80
    A Note of Caution 82
    Avoiding U.S. Excise Tax on Foreign Transfers 83
    Foreign or "Offshore" Corporations 83

Transfers of Property: Is It A Fraud? 86
    The Law of Fraudulent Conveyances: 87
    Intentional Fraud 88
    Creditors' Remedies 89

Swiss Annuities As Alternatives To Trusts 91
    Swiss Annuities and Asset Protection 92
    The Many Added Advantages of Swiss Annuities 94
    A Brief Summary of the Benefits of Swiss Annuities 98
    Protecting Your Assets Through Swiss Annuities 100
    Using A Swiss Insurance Broker 100

The Hybrid Company As An Alternative To The Trust 102

Sources of Help for Offshore Investing 105
    JML Swiss Investment Counsellors 105
    Weber Hartmann Vrijhof & Partners 106

Tax-Free Investing in the United States 109
    American Options Investing 110
    Asset Allocation -- The Key To Successful Investing 114

Last Words 122

Glossary 123

About the Author 133

End Notes 134

Asset Protection Through Swiss Life Insurance Policies

By Marc Sola

OVERVIEW OF ASSET PROTECTION IN SWITZERLAND 136

ANALYSIS OF SWISS ASSET PROTECTION LAWS 139

TREATMENT OF FOREIGN ANNUITIES UNDER U.S. TAX LAW 145

END NOTES 149

Investing Offshore Through Portfolio Bonds

By Marc Sola

How it works 153

Overview of benefits 154

Conclusion 159

Endnotes 161

Offshore Trusts

by
Adam Starchild

Introduction: "Trust Me" -- A Word About Trusts

When we hear the word "trust" it is almost always employed by the speaker to convey a special, distinctive connotation.

Invoking the Deity, "In God We Trust" is the official national motto etched on all U.S. currency and coinage.

People use "trust" to describe a unique personal relationship on which firm reliance rightfully can be placed. Similarly, in the law the definition of "trust" also partakes of a special quality of reliance, high purpose and mutual confidence.

We hope the reader of this book will come away with a thorough understanding of the ancient legal device known as a "trust." Of equal importance, you will be better equipped to make intelligent decisions about your possible personal use of a trust, and the potential benefits a trust can make available to you and your loved ones.

Yet many people seem unaware of the need, but from the personal finance viewpoint each of us should be pursuing two major objectives; the best ways to reduce the government tax bite, and the best means to assure wealth will pass to our intended beneficiaries.

Previously the financial preserve of the rich (if not always the famous), today the trust as a method to achieve these worthwhile objectives has come into its own. There are now few reasons why anyone with sufficient assets to protect or property to pass on should not avail themselves of the time-tested and universally recognized sheltering mechanism that is the trust.

The trust, is one of the most flexible legal mechanisms available, eminently useful for almost any purpose that is not illegal or against public policy. A trust can own and conduct a business; hold title to and invest in real estate, cash, stocks, bonds, negotiable instruments and personal property; care for minors or the elderly; pay medical, educational or other expenses; provide financial support in retirement, marriage or divorce; and serve as a major avenue of avoidance for the muddle of probate courts and the burden of income, inheritance and joint ownership taxes.

By their very nature trusts are relatively complex and technical, a domain of lawyers and accountants, investment planners and bankers, which means there is a definite expense of creation and administration. But do not let complexity or cost dampen your interest. A well-crafted trust can play a major role in your estate, tax, gift and investment planning -- as well as save and earn you and your family lots of money -- far more than it will cost to establish and operate.

In some circumstances, a trust can serve as an excellent asset protection device -- blocking the demands of creditors, ex-spouses and assorted irate litigants bent on taking away your hard-earned property -- and we do live in a highly litigious society.

Although it has ancient Roman and medieval English origins, only in the last half of this 20th century has the trust come to full flower as a practical means of tax avoidance. Mass rearrangement of individual and family assets, multi-jurisdictional property ownership, personal asset protection -- each are major incentives for expansion of trust use, but banking, business and commerce have also invoked the trust concept to attain and promote their own ends.

The day is over when the trust was relegated to the narrow field of wills and estate planning. Trusts have acquired recognized status in the domestic law of many nations, plus an international application that cuts across common law and civil law jurisdictions, without respect to national boundaries.

In these pages we describe and discuss various useful forms of the international asset protection trust with the goal of providing you easy comprehension of trusts, trust law and related tax savings.

A Short History of Trusts

Probably the first and only mention of a "trust" many readers encounter is in a secondary school history text book containing references to 19th century business monopolies known in their day as "trusts."

These were not "trusts" in the sense we consider here, but rather cartels of wealthy corporations formed as an economic alliance to destroy competition and dominate markets. These "trusts," eventually outlawed by the U.S. Congress, were spawned by wealthy men like John D. Rockefeller, the Vanderbilts and Jay Gould, so-called "captains of industry" who joined together with business cohorts to control sales and distribution of products or services -- steel, oil, gas, sugar, railroad, banking.

Such historic monopoly business combinations have no relation to the legal trust, and that popular use of the word should not be confused with the true trust as defined in these pages.

Then again, your first encounter with the type of legal trust we are discussing may have come in a different fashion. Movie buffs may recall old Hollywood drawing room comedies or dramas where some spoiled, rich dandy with a carnation boutonniere seemed to have a "trust fund" that kept him in cash with no need to work for a living. That popular notion of trusts being only for the wealthy, as we said, is now a thing of the past.

An Ancient Custom

The trust concept is rooted in antiquity.

Evidence of the earliest known trust was discovered in an Egyptian tomb, part of a document containing a personal last will and testament written in the year 1805 BC. There were trusts in both Roman and Greek law. The Romans called it *fiducia*, the Latin from which our English word "fiduciary" is derived.

In a sense, the modern trust evolved from the Roman view of property as a distinct entity. The Romans did not have trusts as we know them -- there was no parallel for the modern practice under which a trustee can independently administer and control property for the benefit of another -- but the Romans developed fiduciary systems that accomplished similar purposes in different ways.

The Roman legal concept most closely approximating the trust was the *fiducia*, a device conferring on one person primary obligations for the property of another by mutual consent. The ownership of property was conveyed to a *fiduciary,* who formally agreed to carry out the purpose for which the transfer was made.

The *fideicommissum,* as this transaction was called, underwent extensive elaboration over time. Originally devised as a means of circumventing the rule that only Roman citizens could inherit land, it developed wide use as a method of disposing of property after death. However, the fideicommissum never developed much beyond a substitute ownership arrangement in a testamentary situation.

The First Roman Trust

Roman law first officially recognized the trust idea during the reign of Emperor Augustus Caesar, nearly two thousand years ago. This imperial acceptance of the trust is said to have resulted from the perfidious actions of a deceitful friend who was asked by a wealthy Roman father to act as the trustee of his property in the event of his death. The father's wife was not a Roman citizen and under Roman law both mother and children were prevented from inheriting his property. The concerned father proposed to will his property to his friend in return for a promise to use it only for the benefit of the children. After the father's death, the friend inherited the property but soon betrayed the trust, using the property for his own benefit instead.

This wrong came to the attention of the Emperor who ordered the "trustee" brought before the courts. The judges found the "friend" guilty of a breach of trust, for which he was punished. This ruling was the first recorded judicial approval of the trust in Roman law, and in time the device became so popular, a special court was created to deal exclusively with trust matters.

European Trust Law

Both Germanic and Frankish law also recognized a form of trust in theory, and from the time of Mohammed the concept of the trust was a fundamental principle of Islamic law.

In the Middle Ages, when the quasi-religious Order of Knights Templar acted as Paris-based international bankers and financiers, they employed the trust for royal and ecclesiastical investors who wished to keep secret their financial activity from the public and each other.

Germanic law did not recognize the modern concept of a last will and testament as a device for disposing of property after death. Instead, it was customary for a donor to retain a life interest but convey his property to a *Salmann,* a third party who would dispose of the property at death in accord with the donor's prior instructions. The institution of the Salmann offers a clear precedent for the roles of executor and administrator in English law. The Germans also developed the *treuhänd,* a concept akin to the modern day executorship. Roman precedents were cited to control the activities of a Treuhänder who violated the purpose of his trust, some times curtailing the power to transfer property and permitting the settlor, the creator of the arrangement, to sue for any loss.

The French *hypothec* concept is also comparable to the modern trust since it allowed one person to have a charge or claim on another's property. Third-party hypothecs were used to hold security for a debt, but also played a fiduciary role by safeguarding a person's rights in property. For example, under French civil law a married woman might hold a hypothec over her husband's property, thus protecting her marital rights in that property. A ward had a similar claim on property held by a guardian.

However the 1804 Code Napoleon rejected the English trust idea and instead instituted the French principle of personal absolute property ownership. In most civil law nations there never developed a concept comparable to the trust as English and Americans know it. Established civil law principles such as the "law of obligations" and the "law of property," are not really comparable to the Anglo-American trust, despite confused attempts to portray them as such.

English and American Origins

The roots of the modern Anglo-American trust are deep in feudalistic property concepts established under English common law, virtually free of any Roman law influence.

The trust directly grew out of the medieval English "use," a feudal practice allowing a land owner to transfer his ownership to another who held the title "to the use of" the transferor, or for some other named person or institution. Initially unrecognized at law and therefor unenforceable, the use transferee, the forerunner of today's trustee, had only a moral obligation to adhere to the wishes of the transferor.

Among legitimate functions, a use provided a means of administration, management, sale or disposition of property apart from the person who actually received its benefits. It also served questionable purposes such as defrauding creditors and cheating feudal landlords out of their dues or taxes.

After the anti-clerical regime of the oft-married King Henry VIII, the use allowed banned religious institutions to derive benefits from land they were forbidden to own legally by the Statute of Mortmain. Although originally common law courts refused to approve uses giving ecclesiastical institutions ownership, in the 14th century the Chancery Court responded to church pleas and directed uses be honored, thus allowing the church to collect income from property. By the time the Crown established special "Courts of Conscience" to enforce the use, the device had become a recognized means to convey property for the benefit of another person or institution named by a transferor of land.

The use was probably the world's first tax shelter, allowing beneficial land owners to avoid feudal taxes on property inheritances and transfers. Feudal dues were avoided because the land title holder was not the beneficial owner, monastic vows of poverty were circumvented because the land title was not held by the religious order itself, and the principle of primogenitor, inheritance by the first born, was also avoided by a father creating a trust benefitting other of his children.

In reaction, the Statute of Uses, passed by Parliament in 1535, sought to abolish the use by automatically transferring title in all such property to the true beneficiaries, who then could be taxed directly and held personally responsible for ownership. The major purpose of the Statute was to end a practice by which feudal lords, in particular the King, lost substantial revenues based on a mere legal technicality of beneficial ownership.

Over the next two centuries, however, the use survived the prohibition of the Statute as numerous court decisions crafted it into a recognizable entity we now know as the trust. Judicial rulings concerning the Statute created a great variety of new legal estates in land, as well as new methods of transfer. By 1540, when the Statute of Wills legalized the disposition of land by will, the trust was an accepted part of English law and life.

By the mid-1700s, the Chancery Court, repeatedly using its broad equitable powers, had decided many cases approving the various characteristics of the modern trust. After the American Revolution, these English precedents were adopted as law in the new United States, along with most common law concepts and case decisions existing on Independence Day, July 4, 1776. In this way, the English law of equity, including the trust, became part of the common law of the United States and though considerably modified, remains so to this day.

Because the trust was conceived and embraced in England, it is understandable that the legal system of the British Empire, later the Commonwealth of Nations, sewed the trust concept around the world in all common law nations. Although these national legal systems all share the notion of the trust, that is not to say the trust operates and has the same effect in every country, because it does not. These national trust law differences must be kept in mind when comparing each common law nation and its individual domestic application of trusts.

Trust Evolution

During its lengthy evolution into the modern trust, the use acquired a distinct character of its own, becoming an integral and influential part of English and American family life and society.

The use/trust allowed citizens caught on the losing side in England's civil wars to avoid forfeiture of land based on charges of treason. In a time when married women were unable to own property, the use made it possible for a father to place property in trust for a married daughter.

By degrees, this new trust institution acquired fundamental distinguishing characteristics. The medieval use applied only with respect to land, but the trust encompassed all forms of property, real personal and mixed, and eventually included many forms of commercial activity.

Whereas the medieval use was a passive arrangement, the trust became an active device. Under the use, the *"feoffee"* -- the third person to whom title was transferred -- was expected to allow the beneficiary to control the land. In contrast, the trust usually gives the trustee the right and power to administer the property himself on behalf of the beneficiary.

Charitable Gifts and the Civil Law

The legal systems of civil law nations treat gifts for charitable purposes differently than does Anglo-American common law, imposing more rigorous requirements on donors than those required in the United States or England.

After the Protestant Reformation, trusts replaced the church as the vehicle for a huge development of secular charitable giving, creating distinctions that remain important to this day.

Three choices are generally open to donors making charitable gifts under Anglo-American law. The first is a donation directly to an institution with the donor relying on that institution to fulfill the giver's intentions; secondly, a donor can transfer property to a trustee who reconveys it to the institution; thirdly, donors may establish their own trusts specifically formed to carry out their charitable intentions.

By contrast under civil law, donors usually have only the first of these options, transferring property to an existing institution that accepts an obligation in theory to follow the donor's instructions, the only trust method permitted under old Roman law.

Traces of Roman influence also survive in civil law alternative methods of making charitable gifts. For example, in Germany the Treuhänd concept was expanded with the church becoming the Treuhänder, or administrator of property. The right to create an entity to carry out specific charitable purposes is allowed in modern German law and the *Stiftung,* or foundation, has a corporate structure headed by a board of directors, or Vorstand.

Modern Uses

The 19th and 20th centuries have witnessed a broad expansion of trust use to meet varying objectives well beyond traditional estate planning, embracing marriage, family and elderly care, wealth and asset protection, commercial and social purposes including real estate and investments of all sorts, as well as pension and retirement plans held in trust.

For a family, especially one with some wealth, the trust offers the legal machinery through which the trust creator, the **settlor**, can provide support for successive family members for several generations. (Throughout, we use the term "settlor," although "grantor," "creator," "trustor" and "donor" also are used interchangeably in many texts).

The common law **rule against perpetuities** does not permit perpetual trusts, with the exception of some charitable trusts, but the law permits broad diversity in family trust arrangements, with trust creation either during a settlor's life ("**inter vivos**") known as a "**living trust**", or in testamentary form after death.

A good example of this family use is the **marriage settlement trust**, executed by a living donor, often a parent, to take effect at the settlor's or another family member's marriage. Property is transferred to trustees for the benefit of a husband and wife while both are living, afterward for the benefit of the survivor for the duration of his or her life, and finally the estate is divided among the couple's children or grandchildren as each attains a specific age.

Trusts established under wills -- **testamentary trusts** -- often provide for the sale of part or all of a testator's assets, the proceeds

Using Offshore Trusts, Annuities, and Portfolio Bonds

to be invested in income-producing securities for the benefit of named beneficiaries, usually the surviving spouse and children.

Because a family trust is designed to provide financial security for close relatives, blanket state laws give them special protection, irrespective of whether similar provisions are incorporated in the trust document itself. For example, an **infant beneficiary** lacks legal capacity to hold title to property until the child reaches majority, usually 18 years of age. In the meantime, the law names trustees with discretionary powers over the property, employing them for the infant's maintenance, education, and benefit, whether or not the parents are alive and able to provide support.

Persons of unsound mind or irresponsible habits receive special consideration under modern trust statutes, as do handicapped persons. As in a case of infancy, trustees are empowered to use income and, in some instances, principal for the maintenance and benefit of such persons.

Peculiar to American trust law, persons who demonstrate personal financial irresponsibility, often an adult child, still can be the beneficiaries of a "**spendthrift trust**," the principal of which cannot be legally encumbered by the beneficiary, thus giving immunity from creditors. English and other common law countries have a somewhat different "**protective trust**," that is terminable by law if the beneficiary seeks to encumber it or files bankruptcy.

It is worth noting another major difference between American trusts and those in England and other common law jurisdictions. The latter nations allow **voluntary termination** of a trust by action of adult beneficiaries prior to the trust's stated date for termination, while in America trust beneficiaries have limited termination rights under extraordinary circumstances, usually only after a judicial hearing and decision.

Social and Economic Uses

Today trusts are freely employed for a variety of custodial, social and public purposes by such diverse groups as labor unions, pension plans, social clubs, and philanthropic organizations. In these public uses trustees typically serve as a board of directors, managing the trust and representing the organization to the world at large.

Charitable trusts rank among the most important of those used for social purposes. Named beneficiaries need not be mentioned in the trust instrument; general groups, the public or society as a whole, may be the intended beneficiary of such a trust.

The definition of a charitable trust has proved elusive. A charity in British and American usage usually refers to an educational, religious, or community welfare organization. But because the words *"philanthropic"* and *"benevolent"* have been interpreted as having broader meanings than *"charitable,"* trusts established for "charitable" purposes have in some cases been declared unrecognized at law. Many trusts created for charitable purposes have been aborted by courts, because the trust did not benefit the public generally, or the benefits were divided between charitable and clearly non-charitable objects or beneficiaries. In recent years American courts have nullified some charitable trust provisions held to be discriminatory because of restrictions based on race, sex or economic status.

Commercial Functions

Many years ago a unique form of doing business developed in the Commonwealth of Massachusetts, known as the "Massachusetts trust," about which we will have more to say in chapter 9. We note it here as confirmation that the trust has long performed business functions, much like a corporation in many cases.

Using Offshore Trusts, Annuities, and Portfolio Bonds

Far beyond the function of the business trust, in this century trusts have assumed a major role in commercial life, commonly acting as trustees for group investment plans, clients' bond issues, employee pension plans and, in jurisdictions where the trust tax structure makes it attractive, as business or trading trusts, similar to the Massachusetts trust.

Other developments of the commercial trust include acting as trustee of a business or personal insurance trust, (see chapter 7), a device widely used to minimize taxes. Trust companies also act as third party guarantors for transfers of a business enterprise to one or more beneficiaries, who may be relatives or associates of the business settlor of the trust.

Internationally, the Anglo-American common law trust has been widely accepted, even in civil law nations, as a means of vesting ownership of property in one person for the benefit of another person. It is now formally recognized in the civil-law systems of Liechtenstein, Mexico, Panama, Puerto Rico, Venezuela and such countries as Sri Lanka and South Africa, both with essentially Roman-Dutch systems of law.

In the United States, the trust has become an acceptable means for passing title to property and providing for beneficiaries even in the unique civil-law state of Louisiana, where much of the law is based on the civil Code Napoleon.

Estate Planning

Perhaps the greatest usage of trusts occurs in estate planning as an effective way of passing title to property, while avoiding both lengthy and complicated probate court procedures as well as inheritance taxes. In the United States, probate fees (exclusive of taxes), average from one to 15 percent of the gross value of the entire estate, a enormous sum in many cases. The probate process in some states, like California, can require up to two years to complete.

A trust, especially if operative for several years, provides insulation from attack because it is less likely to be challenged legally compared to a will, which may be more easily contested during probate. And the existence of a trust is an obvious defense to the charge of mental incompetency often used to attack the validity of a will, especially one written late in life.

Asset Protection

As you will see, there are numerous specific types of trusts, each type characterized by different variables included in the trust terms, each with its own degree of potential asset protection, each with its own advantages, problems and tax consequences. At various stages of a person's economic life, one or more of these legal devices may be appropriate, and as circumstances change, new ones may well be needed.

We will examine special foreign and domestic trusts from the prospective of effective asset protection, as well as reduced taxes and assured estate distribution.

Trust Purposes and Principles

Anatomy of a Trust

In order to better understand the creation and operation of a trust in every day life, let us consider the motivations and step through the motions of a person who decides to establish a trust.

Uncle Walt knows he is getting on in years and wants to do something to provide for his favorite nephew, Donald. He gives his life-long best friend, Mickey, 1,000 shares of Disney preferred stock in return for Mickey's agreement to hold the stock in trust and, acting as trustee, reinvest it for the benefit of Uncle Walt's only nephew, Donald, and for Donald's three children, Huey, Dewey and Louie.

The *written trust agreement, or declaration as it is also called,* specifies Mickey as trustee is to pay to Donald, as long as Donald lives, income from the stock or from property purchased with the income produced by Mickey's prudent investment policies. After Donald's death, the property remaining will be given equally to Donald's children.

Uncle Walt is the **settlor**, the person providing the property and creating the trust. Mickey is the **trustee**. *The trust receives* full legal ownership of the trust property, the Disney stock. As trustee, Mickey is the manager with the power and duty to carry out the settlor's wishes as expressed in the **trust declaration** or "indenture" or "agreement," all words used to describe the basic document setting out the details of the trust purpose and operation.

Donald and his children are the **beneficiaries** under the trust. In this trust arrangement Donald also bears the title of *"life tenant,"* because he has the right to receive the income from the trust as long as he lives. His interest is called a *"life estate."* His children are *"remainderman,"* because they have a *remainder* interest, meaning the right to the property when Donald's life estate ends.

Unborn or unknown persons also may be designated as beneficiaries. If Uncle Walt had indicated, for example, that all of Donald's children who were living at Donald's death were to be remaindermen, that could include children not yet born when the trust agreement was signed.

The Disney stock constitutes the ***corpus*** of the trust, also called the *trust property, or "principal."* Here the corpus is stock, but it could be real estate, cash, an existing business, insurance, or any other kind of property. A trust corpus can include any property that can be owned, sold, or otherwise transferred from one person to another.

Which of the elements and people involved in Uncle Walt's trust are indispensable?

Every trust must have five basic components: a settlor, a trustee, a beneficiary, trust property, and some form of governing trust document or agreement.

Because Uncle Walt's trust is established while he is still alive, it is called a "**living trust**". He could have written the trust into his will to take effect when he died, then it would have been a "**testamentary trust**." We will have much to say about both of these kinds of trusts later.

Decisions and a "Declaration"

The prospective trust creator or settlor must make many basic decisions before he or she authorizes the creation of a trust in final form.

Because trust substantive law and tax law is very complex, this is not an area of personal financial planning where the American penchant for "do it yourself" should be indulged. At stake in trust creation is the settlor's valuable property, his or her future well-being, and the economic and personal future of those about whom the settlor cares most, often a spouse and children.

These are not matters to be taken lightly or considered in isolation, and therefore trust creation requires expert legal assistance, professional financial advice and careful tax planning.

Using this book and other informative material, the likely trust settlor should fully acquainted themselves with the many types of trusts available, the purposes of each, and the ultimate outcomes of various different trust provisions. A settlor even should go so far as to obtain the exact mathematical projections based on various percentage pay out rates the trust may allow over a projected number of years and, most certainly, there should be a full computation and understanding of possible tax consequences.

In order to create a trust properly, the well-informed settlor should provide information for, then read, understand, approve and sign a professionally prepared written "**declaration**" or "indenture." This document should reflect the settlor's wishes and the specific details of trust operation and income distribution, both during the settlor's life and after. Numerous court decisions interpreting trust documents have given every clause special meaning, therefore the writing of the trust declaration requires expert advice, as well as assistance and coordination with all other arrangements the settlor may make concerning his or her estate.

Even before the trust declaration is reduced to writing, the settlor must consider and decide upon many important factors to include in this basic document that governs the trust. To wit:

- The trustee and beneficiaries must be named and their rights and responsibilities specifically enumerated with clarity.
- The purpose of the trust must be described, the initial amount and type of property it will contain chosen, and

provision made for property transfer to the trust. There should be provisions governing trust termination, the duration of the trust life, and alternatives tying the termination date to any future events on which trust operation is to be made contingent, such as subsequent births, marriages or deaths.
- The settlor may state conditions a beneficiary must fulfill in order to qualify to receive income from either trust interest or principal, and may limit or expand beneficiary future eligibility based on attained age or other contingencies, such as marriage or income levels. Specific detailed provisions should be included governing distributions of income and principal. Alternative dispositions should be stated in the event trust conditions are not fulfilled, or to govern changed circumstances, as when a beneficiary or trustee dies.
- No trust provisions are of greater importance than setting out the powers and limitations under which the trustee will function, usually allowing a large measure of discretion. In essence, the settlor makes the trustee an extension of himself by granting powers of management and disposition of property comparable to his own power prior to the trust creation.

Judicial Definitions

Let us repeat, in the most basic terms a trust is a fiction recognized by law permitting property, the **corpus**, the legal title to which is held by a person, the **trustee**, who manages it for the benefit of one or more other persons, the **beneficiaries**. Unlimited variations of this simple definition are available, and here are some representatives samples taken from American court cases:

- A "trust is an estate, legal title to which is vested in a trustee, while equitable title is held by individuals who bear no contractual relations among themselves.[1]
- A "trust" is an equitable right, title, or interest in property, real or personal, distinct from the legal ownership thereof.[2]
- A "trust" is an obligation arising out of a confidence reposed in a person, for another's benefit, to apply property faithfully and according to such confidence.[3]
- A "trust" is one of several juridical devices whereby one person is enabled to deal with property for benefit of another person, and among such devices are bailment, guardianship, and agency.[4]

Article II of the Hague International Convention governing trust law and the worldwide recognition of trusts states: ". . . the term 'trust' refers to the leagl relationship created -- inter vivos or on death -- by a person, the settlor, when assets have been placed under the control of a trustee for the benefit of a beneficiary or for a special purpose."

What A Trust Is Not

While these definitions stress what a trust is, it may help to clarify the term by considering what a trust is not.

A trust is *not* an **agency** relationship. In an agency arrangement, the agent represents and acts on behalf of another person, the principal, who chooses the agent. A trustee, on the other hand, receives and personally holds title to and controls trust property, the corpus, acting independently in his or her own trust capacity. In the U.S. a trust may ordinarily be terminated only by fulfillment of its purpose, but an agency usually may be revoked by the principal at any time.

A trust is not a **bailment**, wherein one person, the bailor, entrusts another with his or her personal property, but does not give the property title to the one to whom possession is given, the bailee. Thus, a trust company may act as a bailee, agent, or custodian for another's securities. Bailments are usually created for a short term for a specific, limited purpose as when you leave your clothes at a dry cleaners, but a trust may exist for many years and have many duties, depending on its terms and objectives.

A trust is not the same as an **executorship** or an **administration**, as in the case of a deceased person's estate created by will or by law. Unless otherwise specified, an executor's or administrator's duties involve only the distribution of the deceased person's estate and payment of all debts. Once this is accomplished, the duty ends.

A trust is not a **guardianship,** which is a temporary legal arrangement designed to provide an overseer for a person who is a minor (under the age of 18), or one incapable of caring for himself or managing his own affairs because of mental or physical disability. In most cases a court appoints a guardian based upon a showing of facts supporting the need. A trust can accomplish the limited objects of a guardianship, but a trust usually has much broader duties and is rarely established by a court order, but by a private settlor who creates it voluntarily.

Trust Location

Common sense usually dictates a trust should be located in the place that has the major material connection with the settlor's personal estate. The decisive factor may be the location of real property comprising the corpus of the trust that will require continuing management by a trustee. Often the place of residence of either the settlor or the trustee at the time of trust creation will govern the proper choice.

Using Offshore Trusts, Annuities, and Portfolio Bonds

In this day of migratory international citizens constantly changing residences, the choice of trust location easily can be based solely on a variety of favorable national laws. This allows the settlor an initial choice of the most advantageous law to govern the trust, since it can be created in any national or state jurisdiction.

Some countries are far more flexible than others when it comes to trust law. Each has particularly liberal trust statutes giving much latitude for management by a trustee, and taxes are favorable.

Change of Trust "Situs"

A trust created in one place, fortunately, later can be moved elsewhere.

If one relocates to a new home away from the harsh winters of the north, perhaps in the balmy climate of the Mediterranean, a trust can move with you. This is called a "change of situs." *"Situs"* means the place where the active duties of the trustee are performed.

As a precautionary measure, every trust declaration should contain a clause allowing a change of situs. Often this is accomplished by giving the income beneficiary the right to request the trustee's resignation, and the right to nominate a replacement trustee located in the beneficiary's new community.

In no event should a change of situs be allowed to cause an interruption of the trust existence. The trust legally must be recognized in the new situs as a continuation of the original declaration, wherever it may have been drawn originally. This need for continuity is to avoid serious increased tax consequences that follow the premature termination of a trust.

Choosing a Trust Situs

The decision on where to locate a trust situs, or later, where to move it, should be based on both tax and non-tax reasons.

General Reasons

1. Traditionally trust location should be where the principal beneficiary and/or the trustee lives, but for most offshore and asset protection trusts the primary goal is to locate the trust in a different jurisdiction than one that might have jurisdiction of the principal beneficiary or the settlor. A trust can move from the original jurisdiction to another, along with the beneficiary and/or the trustee.
2. If later a new trustee in a different jurisdiction must be substituted for a former trustee, the situs can be changed.
3. Most nations that cater to foreign trusts are stable and suitable for the situs, but currency devaluation, political instability, or a changed business climate may threaten the viability or security of a foreign trust or its corpus, then change is imperative.
4. A choice of situs may offer lower trustee commissions, custody fees, legal fees, and other costs of services, and if these costs increase, a change may be in order.
5. For trusts formed in the United States, a change to a new trustee in a new state jurisdiction may enable the trust to sue or defend a suit in a federal court, rather than in a state court.

Tax Reasons

1. The original situs choice should take into account taxes imposed on trust income and capital gains paid by local residents. If taxes go up, the situs can go elsewhere.

2. A change of situs may be justified if another jurisdiction exempts the trust from local income tax as a nonresident trust.
3. A foreign trust situs may be rejected or moved to the U.S. when a U.S. citizen is beneficiary to avoid anti-foreign trust and IRS accumulation taxes. (A similar strategy can sometimes work with other high-tax countries.)
4. A trust situs may be chosen in a foreign tax-haven location with low or no trust taxes to avoid taxes of various kinds.

Basics of Trust Creation

The person who creates a trust, variously called the "donor," "grantor" or "**settlor**" (the term we use), conveys legal title to a body of his or her real or personal property or money, the "**corpus**," to a third party, the "**trustee**," perhaps a trusted friend, professional financial manager or a bank with a trust department, to be managed or invested by the trustee for the benefit of a named person or other "**beneficiary**."

A basic feature of the legal concept of a trust is the separation of two ownership interests in a particular property or collection of properties, known as the "corpus." The "**legal title**" to the property is held by the trust and managed by the trustee. The second interest in the same property is the "**equitable title**" held by one or more "beneficiaries," giving them certain rights in the trust corpus known as a "**beneficial interest**."

The relationship between the trustee and the beneficiary is a **fiduciary** relationship, creating special legal obligations of honesty and fair dealing the trustee must fulfill. The trustee has the duty to manage the property not for the benefit of himself, but for the holders of the equitable title. While preserving the trust, a trustee must at all times protect and promote the best interests of the beneficiary as defined in the trust declaration, the charter document.

Under the law, the legal title or ownership of the trust corpus passes from the settlor to the trust. Control and management of these assets is vested in the trustee, so long as the trust exists. Trust property is immune from any personal debts or obligations the trustee may incur, and cannot be attacked by creditors or others who may have personal claims against the trustee.

Powers and duties of a trustee can be broad or narrow according to the trust declaration, but should carefully reflect the settlor's intentions as to how the trust is to be used. The settlor may also be the trustee, or one of the trustees, but such arrangements impose a strict fiduciary duty against self-dealing by the settlor/trustee, lest the validity of the trust itself be called into question. As we discuss more fully below, courts have ruled trusts invalid as a "sham" when a settlor creates a trust, then serves as trustee and is sole beneficiary, simply to avoid personal debts or tax obligations.

The Corpus

What assets should be placed into a trust? That depends entirely on the purpose of the trust -- limited or expansive, specific or general.

One thing is certain: if one goes to the trouble and expense of creating a trust, an argument can be made that all assets should be transferred to the trust. By "funding" the trust (transferring property into it) to the maximum possible extent, the settlor obtains the procedural and tax saving benefits permitted by the trust during life and after death as well.

Many people place great reliance on the fact that much of their property is held jointly with their spouse, an arrangement many do not seem to realize can greatly increase tax liabilities. Joint ownership means that upon one party's death the other automatically inherits the deceased person's interest, but what happens if one of the joint owners is disabled? A court has to be asked to set up a guardianship to manage the joint interest, then real estate and securities can be tied up for months. But if the property is in a trust, the trustee, without further need to seek other authority, can manage the disabled person's property for their benefit during disability.

So the best answer is: fund your trust with all your real and personal property, including jointly held property. Depending on tax consequences, which must be considered carefully, all certificates of stock, securities and other evidences of ownership should be re-issued in the trust name. Cash bank account titles should be changed from your name to that of the trust. The trust can be made the beneficiary of life insurance and in some cases, pension plans. In some jurisdictions the law requires a separate trusts for real estate, but that is only a matter of paper work. Business interests, including corporate ownership and partnership interests can also be placed in a trust, but because of management flexibility, consideration should be given to the creation of a separate trust for business interests.

Certainly before you create a trust you should compile a complete inventory of everything you own. Property suitable for inclusion in a trust at a minimum may consist of:

- All real property a person owns in his or her own name.
- All or part of real property they own with a spouse or other person as joint tenants with right of survivorship.
- The proceeds of life insurance policies on a person's life.
- Pension and profit-sharing benefits.
- Assorted other assets, including personal property.

Remember that until the trust is actually "funded," usually it is not operative in the eyes of the law. The transfer of property into the trust is the trigger that begins trust operation.

"Funding" refers to the act of placing assets in the trust by a formal transfer of title. The revocable living trust, discussed below, can be funded immediately on creation, or later when funds become available. Alternatively, the living trust can have both funded and unfunded portions, as when a settlor immediately places part of his estate in trust, and at the same time provides that proceeds of life insurance policies or employee death benefit plans are to be paid into the trust after his death.

An unfunded portion of a trust estate, also called a "dry trust," can also receive property under the terms of a so-called "pour-over" will drawn in conjunction with the trust agreement, specifying property owned solely by the settlor will be transferred into the trust corpus after death. Making insurance and pension benefits directly payable to the trust, and not to the decedent's estate, wisely exempts these benefits from the claims of creditors, estate administration expenses and inheritance taxes.

The Living Trust

At this point it is advisable to discuss some of the generic characteristics shared by trusts, as well as variations on trust basic themes.

A **living trust** is just what the term indicates, a trust created while the settlor is living (in Latin, an "**inter vivos trust**," meaning "between the living"), serving the twin goals of the settlor's lifetime property control, and directed disposition of trust assets at the settlor's death according to his wishes.

The living trust can offer an answer to many and varying needs related to ownership of real and personal property. Putting property in a living trust can supply new management essential to the proper care or use of that property, including investment experience. It can serve as a shield and support for problems arising from the settlor's or beneficiary's character or situation, such as an owner's inability because of illness or lack of time to administer his property, or a beneficiary's legal infancy. A living trust may be the answer when physical or mental capacity, thrift, interest, maturity, or experience is lacking. The living trust can give the settlor, young or old, the freedom to devote time to business or a profession without interruption or distraction, shifting to the trustee the multiple responsibilities connected with property management.

Among the purposes for a living trust is the desire to *build an estate, as when a young person "on the way up" creates a small living trust with the intent of adding to it over time.* A prudent businessman *may wish to keep his personal wealth independent from his business; the c*reation of a living trust can limit the risk and insulate non-business property from business creditors.

An older person or couple approaching retirement age may wish to have such a trust to *obtain expert administration and management of property,* allowing them the freedom to travel, pursue a hobby or avocation, or launch a new and different retirement business.

In many instances the impetus for trust creation is a family situation, *the possible "rainy day" need to provide a spouse* enough property to yield income for family and personal expenses. Rather than make an outright gift to a son or daughter, a parent may set up a living trust or it can be established for persons other than spouses and children, like parents, brothers, sisters, more distant relations, and friends. A family trust with professional management can supply family members *a missing element of skill in the care, management, or use of property.* For example, a widowed mother can place most of her estate in an irrevocable living trust to prevent her profligate son from constantly importuning her for money.

Advantages and Disadvantages

A living trust, in contrast to a testamentary trust created after the settlor's death under the terms of a will, takes effect and operates immediately while the settlor is alive. Some settlors show wisdom by avoiding a testamentary trust, deciding instead to create a living trust making it possible to familiarize a professional trustee with the details of the estate and the members of the family who are beneficiaries.

In a great many cases, a living trust is little more than a substitute for a will, and both have the attractive feature of being susceptible to change or outright revocation at any time the settlor so desires. But the major advantage a living trust enjoys that a will does not is it removes a settlor's assets from the tangle of probate, although at death there are still federal and state estate taxes with which to contend.

Escaping probate is no small blessing. Disposing of property through a will always ties up the property for months, if not years. In the United States, research in all 50 states showed the average probate time was from six months to a year. A local probate court appoints an executor or administrator who collects the estate properties, holds them until all creditors' claim are filed and settled, files all sorts of required forms and documents, and finally gets around to distribution to heirs.

The average cost of administering a trust is less than one percent of the total value of the corpus. By stark contrast, probate costs generally average from 3 to 8 percent of the total value of the estate. In California, for example, probate fees are charged for any estate gross value of $60,000 or more. In dollars and cents these percentages mean an estate valued at $100,000 will cost about $5,000 to settle; $15,000 for a $400,000 estate; $30,000 for a million dollar estate. A living trust can greatly reduce such costs, even though start up costs may be more; writing an average will costs about $300; creating a simple trust will cost $750 to $1,250.

Trusts: Revocable and Irrevocable

The terms *"revocable"* and *"irrevocable"* describe important distinctions between the two basic types of living trusts.

Within these two categories are many variations classified according to when the trust is created, who benefits, how assets are distributed, or any number of other factors. Trusts do not fall into neat categories because they can serve multiple purposes and their structure reflects that diversity.

First, a matter of definition: "**revocation**" refers to the power of a settlor to cancel a living trust and take back his or her property. "**Termination**" refers to the power of beneficiaries to bring the trust to an end by agreement of all parties concerned or by court action. A few U.S. states follow the English rule and allow beneficiaries to terminate the trust with court approval; most U.S. states prohibit termination except in extraordinary circumstances.

When the settlor retains the power to revoke, alter or amend the trust, it is automatically classified as "revocable." Where no such powers are retained by the settlor under the terms of the trust agreement, the trust is considered "irrevocable."

If a trust declaration is silent on the issue of revocation, the law of the jurisdiction where the agreement was drawn, the situs, will usually determine the question. In most jurisdictions the law assumes a trust is irrevocable if the instrument is silent about revocation powers. In a few jurisdictions, a trust is presumed revocable unless the instrument contains a specific provision to the contrary.

The wise trust settlor never leaves such an important question to chance. They make sure the trust declaration specifically addresses the issue of revocation power one way or the other.

The Revocable Living Trust

The **revocable living trust**, then, is an entity to which a settlor voluntarily transfers title to his or her assets, but with "a string attached." When a trust is "revocable," the settlor retains power during his or her lifetime to vary trust terms, withdraw assets, or even end the trust entirely by formal revocation. Obviously, upon the death of the settlor, a revocable living trust immediately becomes irrevocable, and under its terms is thereafter administered by the trustee for the benefit of the residual beneficiaries or the remaindermen.

There are real benefits to a revocable living trust, the most obvious being the settlor's ability to manage the trust assets during lifetime with the continuing option to end the trust whenever changed circumstances dictate. It is an estate plan that can also be a very beneficial lifetime financial plan for the settlor.

There is no legal prohibition against a settlor serving as trustee and being a life beneficiary also, so long as there are one or more other residual beneficiaries after the settlor's death. In fact, this arrangement is very common. But as a general rule, this game of same settlor/trustee/sole beneficiary can open the entire arrangement to creditor assault in court and negative tax collector scrutiny.

While the settlor usually receives no real immediate additional financial benefits from a living trust, there can be many indirect advantages, such as shifting expenses for medical, educational and other family costs to an entity which is legally insulated against outside attacks, or at least more difficult and costly for creditors to pursue.

But for a spouse or heirs as beneficiaries there are many benefits to the living trust, in addition to acquiring immediate income from trust assets. These advantages include eventually avoiding judicial probate with attendant expense and time delays, since trust property is not included in the settlor's personal estate; allowing the uninterrupted post mortem operation of a family business placed in trust; avoiding probate in more than one jurisdiction if real estate involved is located in two or more jurisdictions; avoiding public scrutiny of personal financial matters and any temporary gap in beneficiaries' income during probate.

Lack of Asset Protection

The one great disadvantage with a revocable living trust is that it provides very little asset protection, especially if the settlor is also the sole beneficiary during life, a cozy arrangement sure to be challenged by creditors, probably successfully. But if the settlor has relative immunity from creditor attack during life, the living trust has accomplished the attractive goal of probate avoidance.

Trust laws generally restrict the nature and extent of benefits and control that a settlor can retain after creating his or her own trust. This is reflected in a principle of trust law stating that when a settlor retains any major degree of control over assets allegedly transferred to a trust, those assets may remain within ultimate reach of the settlor's creditors.

Great reliance is placed on this legal principle by courts examining actual trust operation and this test has upset even the best-intentioned trust plans. The major charge made by creditors against a settlor who creates his or her own trust, one to which courts are sympathetic, is the trust is a smoke screen to avoid payment of just debts or judgments.

In ten U.S. states laws state that a settlor who retains an absolute power of revocation is deemed to be the owner of the trust property for the purpose of creditors and purchasers. These include Alabama, Indiana, Kansas, Michigan, Minnesota, North Dakota, Ohio, Oklahoma, South Dakota, and Wisconsin. Case law in many other states has opened revocable trust arrangements to similar creditor attachment.

Sure Asset Protection

While one revocable living trust may not do it, the right combination of living trusts can provide strong asset protection, in spite of the statutes and court decisions just mentioned placing great emphasis on revocability.

If two revocable living trusts are created, one for each spouse, the spouse engaged in a profession or business that is particularly vulnerable to law suits (and who is not, these days?), can transfer to the other spouse's trust title to their home and personal property that otherwise might be open to business judgment creditors. Repeatedly courts have upheld the separate nature of a spouse's own acquired property from the other spouse's creditors, unless such transfers are obviously done to defraud creditors. If this transfer is made at a time when there are no looming creditors, a spouse's trust is virtually unchallengeable later even if such demands do arise.

In the United States, the law has relieved the property of either spouse from responsibility for the other's separate debts incurred during marriage. And a wife's revocable living trust is her personal property, thus immune from attack for her husband's obligations. Note that we are talking about more than just putting property "in the spouse's name" to protect assets, but rather having title passed to the spouse's living trust, a far more secure position should a court start scrutinizing assets at the behest of irate creditors.

Irrevocable Living Trusts

A living trust also may be expressly created as **irrevocable**, permanently denying a settlor the ultimate control over assets transferred to the trust once established. Irrevocability is the major disadvantage -- if circumstances change, the trust cannot be changed to meet them.

On the other hand, as a protection against creditor asset attachment, this is virtually perfect because the settlor no longer holds title to the property, nor does he have any ability to re-acquire it. The only possible successful attack by creditors might occur if the transfer of property to the trust can be proven fraudulent in some way, usually if it occurs after creditor attacks begin. Irrevocability is the trust's unique feature and a court finding it will usually rule trust assets are shielded from the settlor's creditors.

There are other factors that strengthen an irrevocable living trust as an asset protection device. These include having a legitimate reason for trust creation, apart from simple avoidance of creditors demands, and that may be logical estate planning or reasonable provision for a spouse and children. But one must be careful.

Take for example the case of a grandfather creating an irrevocable trust in which his son is given a life estate and all of a son's children are designated as remaindermen, including the son's much loved step-daughter, the natural child of the son's wife's first marriage. Ten years later the son is divorced, the step-child is long gone living with the ex-wife and her new, third daddy, on the other side of the world. The irate settlor may well want to write the step grandchild out of the trust, but he can't -- it's irrevocable.

In an irrevocable trust, the exercise of trustee powers should be independent, and trust terms should not allow distribution of income to the settlor as a sole beneficiary. Thus courts have held that while a third person may do so, a settlor cannot set up his own "spendthrift trust" immune from creditors. Any distribution of trust assets at the settlor's death should go to a designated class of beneficiaries, usually the spouse and children. The settlor should not serve as the trustee, but a completely independent trustee should be chosen.

In other words, the irrevocable trust must be real in every sense, not just a fake arrangement allowing the settlor a life-long free ride from judgment creditors.

It is worth noting that many courts -- and now more than a few legislatures -- have begun to measure the vulnerability of trust assets in strict terms of a trust's revocability. Since 1987 for example, California statutes have allowed creditors to reach trust assets to the extent a settlor retains power to revoke the trust, and to reach trust payments to a settlor who is also a beneficiary.

Comparative Tax Advantages for American Settlors

Each type of living trust has different tax consequences for the settlor who creates them.

An irrevocable living trust generally is not considered part of the settlor's taxable estate, if he or she does not retain the right to receive trust income or otherwise retain control. This trust is a separate tax entity that pays taxes on its own income, but the settlor does not. Understand that this type of trust can be subjected to high tax rates on undistributed income, and moving personal assets into such trusts can have gift tax consequences in the U.S. (or other countries with gift taxes in which a settlor may reside).

The 1993 U.S. federal tax law revision raised taxes on trust income nearly 30 percent, erasing the previous tax advantage of shifting income to a trust. The new law set the rate of taxation on trust income beginning at 15 percent up to $1,500, and rising to 39.6 percent on income of $7,500 or more. The law also allows future automatic adjustment of these tax brackets to account for inflation.

By comparison to the separate income tax status of an irrevocable living trust, income from a revocable living trust is generally included as part of the settlor's personal taxable income.

Depending on the nature and degree of the powers a settlor reserves over the trust, he or she will be considered owner of the trust under the Internal Revenue Code interpretations, and trust income is counted as taxable personal income. This type of trust is thus invisible for tax purposes; any taxable events are reported on the personal tax forms of the person who sets up the trust. This trust needs no separate taxpayer ID number (the settlor's own Social Security number is used) and does not file separate tax return.

Under the law, the income and assets of a revocable or irrevocable trust are both subject to state and federal death taxes. But these trusts can be arranged so that upon the subsequent deaths of named beneficiaries or their heirs, further death taxes can be avoided, a real savings for the trust beneficiaries, although the benefit of this tax savings is not immediate for them.

For example, the living trust can realize significant tax savings, especially if two trusts are created, one by each spouse for the benefit of the couple's children. Dual martial trusts can be structured to give the surviving spouse the benefit of the other spouse's trust until the survivor dies, then both trusts can continue for the children, or the assets can be distributed to them. Two trusts can split the total trust income and thus reduce trust income and estate taxes, but this is impossible unless different beneficiaries are named for each trust. If more than one trust exists with the same beneficiaries, all of the trusts are lumped together for trust income and estate tax purposes.

Using the $600,000 federal estate tax exemption available to each parent, $1.2 million in death taxes can be avoided, as compared to an inheritance tax of $300,000 or more on a non-trust estate of comparable size received as a straight inheritance. Under federal tax law steeply graduated levies rise to an expropriatory 55 percent for estates valued over $3 million.

Again we emphasize the great importance of creating and operating a living trust within the strict letter of the law. Title to property must be deeded to the trust, and the trustee must manage assets for the benefit of the named beneficiaries. All transactions must be formally correct and records carefully maintained. We repeat, a substantial body of case law backs many successful IRS challenges of defective trusts as no more than evasive devices to avoid tax liability, the one factor courts scrutinize most closely.

Once the IRS rules a trust to be a sham, all the supposed tax advantages disappear, and worse still, back taxes, penalties and interest may be owed in large amounts.

The Testamentary Trust

Once the most common form of trust used in the United States, the still popular **testamentary trust** is a prospective arrangement a testator or testatrix creates as part of his or her will to take effect after death, usually funded by all or part of the property in the decedent's estate.

This method allows provision for loved ones, especially when the testator is concerned about a minor child's ability to manage his or her own affairs, giving rise to the testamentary creation of the so-called "spendthrift trust," the assets of which are immune from attacks by the offspring-beneficiary's creditors.

The testamentary trust has the same characteristics of a living trust and must have the five basic elements of any trust: a creator or settlor, one or more trustees, a beneficiary, property as corpus, and trust terms. A testamentary trust may be implied by law even if a testator does not use the word *"trust"* in the will, if and when a clear intent to create a post mortem trust is shown by all the will's terms and circumstances.

A testamentary trust becomes effective only when a trustee is named; if the will does not designate a trustee by name, the trustee will usually be appointed by the probate court. Two or more trustees may serve together, and both individuals and corporations can act as trustees. As in other trusts, the beneficiaries may be persons, corporations, associations, or other groups capable of property ownership.

In order to become operative, a testamentary trust must receive property of some kind to form the corpus, either title to a valuable legal or equitable interest. The proceeds of a life insurance policy insuring the decedent's life, or any other property can be placed in trust by will. Of course the will should clearly set forth the terms of the testamentary trust, including the duties and powers of the trustee and the purposes for it is created.

While popular, testamentary trusts have distinct disadvantages often unexplained by legal advisors; unlike a living trust, estate and income taxes must be paid at the death of the testator, although successive estate tax levies often can be avoided as trust property passes to beneficiaries and their heirs in later years.

Testamentary trusts cannot avoid initial probate and may be subjected to continuous court supervision, often with huge legal expenses and administration fees. Because they are subject to probate, the activity of the testamentary trust and its trustee is a matter of public record for all to see. All these post mortem problems can easily be avoided by creating a living trust, but old habits die hard and many people demand testamentary trusts. Lawyers should know better.

Express and Implied

In addition to trusts created by wills, trusts can be created formally by contract between two or more parties ("**express trusts**"). When title to real or personal property is involved along with a purchase money mortgage, a "**deed of trust**" is used in many states allowing a third party to hold title until the terms of the mortgage are fulfilled by payment. An "**implied trust**," also called a "constructive trust," may result even in the absence of a formal trust, when a court finds its creation from factual circumstances such as when one spouse consistently buys property with his or her funds, then places it in the name of the other spouse.

It Takes Getting Used To

Admittedly there is something strange at first about "surrendering" everything you own to a "trust," but that feeling will pass quickly once full understanding of trusts and trust operation is achieved. Especially in the case of a settlor who also serves as trustee, all the attributes of property ownership remain, including control and management of that property even though it is titled to the trust.

And for those who value privacy, the living trust affords a shield from "prying eyes" and adversaries who might otherwise contest a will during probate. The creation of a trust can be done in such a way that while its existence is a matter of public record, the names of the settlors and beneficiaries are kept private -- and trust assets need not be disclosed.

In our next chapter we will discuss the parties to a trust, their duties and their powers.

Using Offshore Trusts, Annuities, and Portfolio Bonds

Parties, People, Powers

In this chapter we discuss the people, or as the law describes them, "the **parties**" who are involved in the creation and operation of a trust, theirs powers, duties and rights.

The Settlor

A trust does not just materialize out of thin air. Some person has to make it happen. In our example in chapter 2, no trust would have come into existence if Uncle Walt had not taken the initiative to create the trust. Uncle Walt is the **settlor** of the trust, also variously called the "grantor," "donor" or "trustor," all words you will find in trust literature, all meaning the same thing.

Earlier we mentioned "express" and "implied" trusts, pointing out that there is more than one method by which a trust can come into being.

In our example, other than formally placing legal title to the Disney stock in a trust run by his buddy, Mickey, Uncle Walt could have established a legal trust in several ways -- by oral statements, in writing, or by his conduct. In this case he wisely chose to create the trust with a written declaration naming the trustee and beneficiaries, describing the corpus, and dictating the terms. With the trust in writing, there is not much room for misunderstanding Uncle Walt's intentions.

Had there been no written document, a valid trust still might have been created. In considering proof of an intention to create a trust, a court gives consideration to the words used, the circumstances surrounding the transaction and the actions of the parties. When actions alone indicate intent to create a trust, the law calls it an "implied trust."

Settlor/Trustee as Beneficiary

A trust must have at least one trustee, in our example, uncle Walt chose his long-time friend, Mickey. In every trust there always must be some person or corporate entity given the right and duty to manage or administer the trust in accordance with the terms of the declaration.

Often a trust will have two or more "co-trustees," each with equal powers, meaning any trustee can veto the decision of the other. A trust declaration may also name a "successor trustee" to take over in case an original trustee dies or is allowed to resign -- a trustee cannot usually withdraw unless the trust declaration permits this, or unless a court approves.

As we saw in chapter 2, in certain kinds of trusts the settlor who creates the trust can serve as his own trustee, and can even be the life beneficiary as well, but again we must inject a note of caution.

Under U.S. law, supported by many court decisions, when a settlor also acts as trustee and is the sole beneficiary of the trust ("three-in-one" as it were), the resulting "trust" is very likely to be declared void, at least for tax purposes, as a matter of law. This can happen by a challenge in court, or it can occur as a result of an IRS ruling on the tax status of the trust. Other jurisdictions tend to come to a similar legal conclusion regarding such trusts.

Trust law generally restricts the nature and extent of the benefits and control a settlor can retain after creating a trust for which he or she is also the sole beneficiary. The law states that when a settlor retains any significant degree of control over property transferred to a trust he creates, those assets may be considered to continue as the settlor's personal assets and may remain within reach of the settlor's personal creditors. In other words, a person is not allowed to create a trust as a gimmick to insulated his or her property and avoid just obligations owed to others.

Using Offshore Trusts, Annuities, and Portfolio Bonds

As we noted in chapter 2, ten U.S. states have laws stating a settlor who retains an absolute power of revocation (the so-called **"revocable living trust,"**) is deemed to be the personal owner of the trust property for the purpose of creditors and purchasers.

Does this mean that a settlor should not serve as trustee and be a beneficiary as well? Certainly not.

Lawyers who should know better often tell clients the settlor/client should not serve as trustee of their own living trust, especially if they are also the sole beneficiary. Undoubtedly such an arrangement will receive a hard look from the tax authorities, but if the declaration is properly drafted and there are residual beneficiary waiting at the end of the settlor's life estate, the trust should be safe and sound in the eyes of the law.

As a practical matter, it is highly advisable for the settlor to be his or her own trustee if the trust is created to provide the settlor a life estate. Trust law permits this arrangement -- so long as the trust provides for some other beneficiary after the settlor's death. But that post mortem beneficiary is highly important to avoid having the trust fail in the eyes of the law or the tax authorities.

It is also important to designate in the trust declaration a **"successor trustee"** who will take control in the event of the settlor/trustee's incapacity or death. In large estates, IRS tax rules usually require a successor trustee to be independent, and often this means a spouse or child cannot qualify for the job. In the case of a smaller estate of $600,00 or less, family members usually can qualify as trustee under IRS rules.

For example, in many living trusts the settlor will serve as trustee administering the trust for his and his wife's benefit during his lifetime. At his death, his wife will be the successor trustee during her lifetime, managing the trust for her own benefit. When she dies, one of their children can be successor trustee with the directed duty of dividing the remaining trust property and distributing it among his or her brothers and sisters.

Choosing a Trustee

Perhaps no single decision regarding a trust is of greater importance than the choice of the trustee.

Whether the settlor chooses an individual or corporate entity, the character of the trustee will spell success or failure of a trust and its stated objectives.

The trustee must have unquestioned integrity and a genuine understanding and concern for the welfare of the beneficiaries. A trustee's characteristics should include broad life and business experience and a record that negates the possibility of neglect or incompetence. There must be a genuine sense of responsibility, no reluctance and an absolute willingness to serve. Personal circumstances should permit a trustee to be readily available most of the time.

An Individual Trustee

Which is better as trustee, a relative or friend you know, or a professional trust corporation?

Here are some of the points favoring a non-professional individual as trustee, an individual personally known to the settlor who provides empathy and understanding. A family member, relative, or personal friend may possess all the needed qualifications of a trustee, including investment expertise, accounting skills, and tax know-how. The choice of someone close to the settlor and beneficiaries means the trustee will have personal knowledge of their idiosyncrasies, needs, strengths, and weaknesses.

A personal friend also may discharge a trustee's duties for little or no payment, but all of these factors could be rendered meaningless if the individual has hidden motives or lacks the necessary qualifications. Personal knowledge and opinions about the beneficiaries also can lead to biased or prejudicial decisions.

A Corporate Trustee

There are many strong considerations supporting the choice of a professional trustee. For one thing, professional trust companies are chartered and regulated by the state. Because they want to preserve their good reputation, they are unlikely to run off with their trust client's money. Then too, the range of duties a trustee must discharge requires a depth of knowledge and expert approach in areas such as investing, accounting, and law. A bank trust department or other corporate trustee has such knowledge and skills readily available at all times. Corporate trust officers have access to sound investment information an individual trustee often cannot easily obtain. A personal trust officer receives daily reports on the performance of stocks and bonds, and their brokers and advisors have the continuing duty of counseling trust officers on the best trust investments.

The firm serving as trustee, usually a banking and trust company, has staff members trained to combine skilled advice and counsel with a sympathetic ear, and their detached judgments can remain unclouded by personal bias. A professional corporate trustee offers continuity, stability, and reliability with constant availability.

If participation of a family member in the trust management is considered important, the settlor can name a relative or friend as co-trustee along with a professional trustee. A surviving spouse can be named to serve in that role as well.

On balance, a professional trustee usually is the better choice.

Co-Trustees

A trustee's powers vest when property has been transferred, creating the corpus and once responsibilities are undertaken. If there are two or more co-trustees, the powers vest in both or all jointly.

Except in the case of a charitable trust with a governing board of trustees that acts by majority vote, co-trustees act collectively as equal joint tenants in order to make valid decisions, defend against lawsuits, vote on corporate stock, or take other significant actions. This requirement for collective action is often raised as an objection to naming co-trustees, since it can be cumbersome. A settlor can simplify the task by specifying in the trust declaration methods by which disagreements among the co-trustees are to be resolved.

Where there are co-trustees, if one trustee is unable to discharge his functions, the others can act during the disability. Where there is a single trustee, his death or incapacity allows his successor to assume all powers, express or implied.

Duties of a Trustee

While the trust as an entity holds title to all property, the trustee is effectively the de facto owner exercising all normal incidents of ownership, and providing management of the corpus, including the power to invest and re-invest assets. He is duty bound to use trust property exclusively for the benefit of the beneficiaries.

Court enforceable duties are assigned to a trustee, and under U.S. law only a trustee's "breach of trust" such as failure to act ("**misfeasance**") or improper action ("**malfeasance**"), subjects the trust to court-ordered "execution," meaning ending the trust and transfer of full legal title of the corpus to the equitable beneficial owners.

The trustee is entitled to a fee for his services, normally his only payment for exercising trust duties.

Over centuries courts have incorporated into the law of the United States and common law countries a large body of equitable rules controlling and defining the administrative authority of active trustees, for the most part focusing on investment policy. Protocols exist governing trustees' power to sell, lease, or mortgage trust property, promote the best interests of beneficiaries, the appointment of agents and delegation of authority.

More recently, statutory and case law has held trustees personally liable for failure to advance the best interests of beneficiaries, including imposing a continuing duty to make the best possible trust investments with the highest return. These duties of a trustee include, among other things, selling at the best price possible the assets transferred to the trust; investing the proceeds from the sale in the manner that will best advance the trust goals; arranging cash flow needed for periodic distributions to beneficiaries; annual evaluation of trust assets; filing trust tax forms (if the trust is not located in a tax haven); maintaining a trust bank account and accurate records of income, expenses, payouts and accumulations of income and capital gains; and, informing beneficiaries of how they must personally report annual payouts for their own personal tax purposes.

The first duty of a trustee upon accepting appointment is to take control and protect the trust estate. If he delays, he may be liable for any losses attributable to that delay. Because a trustee cannot delegate basic duties, he personally must make certain adequate insurance coverage exists to protect trust interests. Property taxes must be paid. Stock subscription rights may have to be exercised.

If legal actions are pending against the trust, the trustee must take necessary defensive action. If trust claims against others exist, he is obliged to press all demands, even to bring suit, if required to preserve or protect trust property. If he fails to bring such action, he may be held accountable for what the law calls "careless forbearance."

In discharging his duties under the trust agreement, the trustee acts as would the holder of legal title. He is personally liable for his actions. In exercising his duties and powers a trustee is always theoretically subject to the watchful jurisdiction of the equity court, to which beneficiaries can complain.

A trustee owes an undivided and absolute duty to preserve and enhance the value of trust property, well beyond simple an exercise of simple honesty. He is forbidden to profit or gain advantage from the use or exchange of trust property, to sell or lease trust property to himself, or sell his own property to the trust. One major exception to rules against self-dealing is allowed when the trust declaration establishes interrelated family trusts with language specifying trustees, often family members in such cases, can enter into certain transactions.

Because a trustee is given a position of personal confidence, the trustee cannot generally delegate basic management duties, but may delegate the performance of administrative details. In considering the issue of proper delegation, courts will look to the trust declaration for the amount of discretionary power conferred on a trustee. It is well established that a trustee cannot delegate the power to invest and reinvest, but a trustee has been held to act properly when obtaining and paying for professional investment advice, so long as he exercises reasonable care when selecting that counsel.

A trustee has a positive duty to segregate and identify trust property since the corpus must be administered as an organized collection of assets. For efficiency the trustee identifies and marks trust property, separating it from his own and all other properties that may be involved. A separate, identified trust bank account is a necessity. Securities should be deposited in a special safe-deposit box and contents identified as trust property.

In some cases, the terms of a trust may allow commingling of the assets of two or more trusts, but only by explicit reference and with strict accounting. The intent of the trustor controls in such a case, but the trustee must retain the capacity to prove he has productively and faithfully managed the trust fund. If commingling entails any risk, the trustee must avoid it.

The terms of the trust declaration can make any requirement either more or less stringent, imposing a heavier obligations in some areas of trustee conduct. In others, an exculpatory clause or permissive language may relieve the trustee of strict adherence to a rule.

As a matter of law, courts make certain assumptions regarding a trustee's conduct including the prima face finding that a trustee acts fraudulently if he benefits from a transaction with a trust beneficiary. This principle does not prevent a trustee from acting as attorney, broker, or counsel for a beneficiary in nontrust matters.

Within certain limits the provisions of a trust can supersede laws concerning the standards of conduct of a trustee, but they cannot exonerate him from liability for willful negligence, misconduct or the failure to exercise reasonable care and prudence.

Trustee Powers, Express and Implied

A trustee has both express and implied powers, the former explicitly granted in the trust declaration. As a matter of construction and interpretation, a court presumes implied powers exist where necessary or appropriate for the efficient and proper administration of a trust. Also as a rule, powers not granted explicitly are considered as withheld.

At times a power logically may be implied by the terms of the trust declaration. For example, the corpus may consist of a single piece of valuable real estate, while the trust terms require the trustee to divide the entire corpus among several beneficiaries. This gives the trustee the implied power to convert the asset into cash by selling the real estate in order to carry out the distributive command of the declaration.

A trustee's exercise of true discretionary powers generally remains immune from judicial interference, because a court usually will not substitute its judgement for that of a trustee.

Because management of a trust corpus can and normally does require the trustee to buy, sell, and invest, he generally is given the power of sale. Most trust instruments dealing with assets of any complexity will grant that power by specific provision, along with the *power to borrow, pledge, or mortgage* trust.

A trustee has a general *power to compromise* claims against or owned by the trust and he may submit claims to arbitration, but he may have to justify a compromise as being reasonable.

The power to contract and incur expenses are part of the trustee's general ability to act on behalf of the trust corpus. The trustee is able to exercise the normal rights of a stockholder in dealing with securities, bonds or other negotiable instruments. Management duties and powers also include the express or implied power to lease.

The "Prudent Investor" Rule

The law requires a trustee to exercise "reasonable care and skill," a fairly elusive standard generally meaning the care and skill a prudent person of discretion and intelligence would exercise in similar circumstances.

However this standard has been greatly refined by the courts when it comes to investments. The American "prudent investor" rule governing discretionary investments of trust funds by a trustee dates back to the venerable case of *Harvard College v. Amory*, decided by the Supreme Judicial Court of Massachusetts in 1830.[5] A typical statement of the prudent-man rule reads:

> In acquiring, investing, reinvesting, exchanging, retaining, selling, and managing property for the benefit of another a fiduciary shall exercise the judgment and care, under the circumstances then prevailing, which men of prudence, discretion, and intelligence exercise in the management of their own affairs, not in regard to speculation but in regard to the permanent disposition of their funds, considering

the probable income as well as the probable safety of their capital.[6]

Until 1937, this rule was applied by U.S. courts in only six states, but now is statutory law in 41 states. Nine states (Alabama, Alaska, Arizona, Georgia, Indiana, Iowa, Montana, Nebraska, Wyoming) and the District of Columbia limit investment discretion by imposing specific statutory restrictions on the type of investments legally appropriate for trust funds. Some tax haven jurisdictions have their own version of the prudent-man rule, but many of them allow a wider latitude in drafting a trust document that gives the trustee greater discretion.

As you consider the role of the trustee, keep in mind a trustee often must act in a fiduciary capacity on behalf of the interests of both parties to a trust -- the beneficiary and the remainderman, as in the case of Uncle Walt's trust for Donald and his sons. This means an impartial administration of trust assets to provide both favorable current income, and also preservation of the largest possible remaining corpus for the life beneficiary and the ultimate remaindermen.

The Third Restatement of the Law of Trusts, section 227, the authoritative U.S. treatise on such matters (and sometimes used as guidance in other jurisdictions), imposes a duty on a trustee to manage a trust as a "prudent investor," balancing the rights of the beneficiary and the remainderman in light of the terms of the trust declaration, payout requirements and all other circumstances including inflationary considerations.

The difficulty arises when market conditions make it impossible to satisfy both parties' best interests. Then the trustee is expected to look for direction to the settlor's intent as expressed in the trust declaration -- yet another reason the drafting of that basic document is of such great importance. The question then becomes, did the grantor intend to favor the remainderman over the current income beneficiary? Under the codified Third Restatement rules, a trustee would rarely implement an investment policy that clearly favors one side over the other, unless the trust declaration unambiguously directed such a course. This is so because the Restatement suggests that a trustee can be held personally financially responsible for investing in a manner that favors the beneficiary at the expense of the remainderman, especially if the diminished principal loses purchasing power due to inflation.

For example, a trust arrangement that allows the beneficiary to receive payment out of principal when current income is insufficient, clearly harms the interest of the remainderman -- an inherent conflict of interest for a trustee. This dilemma can be avoided so long as the overall rate of return (current income plus capital appreciation) meets the payout requirement, thus keeping the corpus intact. But when the trustee must figure in inflation, trust principal may have to be invaded to pay the beneficiary.

The practical solution is to set the payout rate named in the trust declaration as low as possible, so that an experienced trustee's wisely diversified portfolio of investments can earn interest and dividends sufficient to meet all current income needs with inflation taken into account.

Trust Investor Rule Update

In New York, as of January 1, 1995, the Prudent Investor Act took effect, joining Illinois and a dozen other states that have adopted this somewhat more liberal law on trust investment. A statutory project of the National Commission on Uniform State Laws, the law softens the older requirement that preservation of capital, and thus risk avoidance, be the primary goal of trust investment policy.

The new law instructs a trustee to invest with an eye to overall return, taking into account inflation and general economic trends, instead of limiting investment to the safest possible investments with the least chance of capital loss. The law places emphasis on a trustee's investment conduct, as compared to the actual investment performance in dollars as a measure of adherence to duty. It also allows a trustee to delegate investment activity to professionals, so long as he maintains oversight. This new approach will allow beneficiaries to demand, and a trustee to provide, a more aggressive trust investment strategy that meets the need for income, rather than just preservation of principal.

In the midst of all these shifting variables, the "prudent investor" trustee can easily get caught "in the middle." These problems should suggest how important it is to choose a qualified trustee who, in fact, has your complete trust.

Guidelines for Trustee Investments

There are accepted guidelines followed by trustees in making trust investments in stocks, bonds, and other assets. For example, trustees apply one standard when investing in marketable securities, another when buying nonmarketable securities. Factors to be considered are:

1. Marketability or liquidity of an investment.
2. The maturity, call, or redemption date of an investment.
3. The probable duration of the trust.
4. The probable condition of the market at trust termination, as that might affect the value of the investment.
5. For reinvestment purposes, the probable condition of the market at the maturity date of the investment.
6. The total size of the corpus and the nature and extent of other investments.
7. Both the beneficiaries' income requirements and their other assets, including income and earning capacity.
8. The tax aspects of any investment.
10. The age of each beneficiary.
11. Family and other circumstances or qualifications.

Support for the Beneficiary

Other than restrictions on investment policy, there are also firm rules governing how a trustee is to use both income and principal for the beneficiary's advantage.

The trustee must pay out support and maintenance sums at reasonable intervals directly to a beneficiary. The trust declaration usually gives a trustee discretionary power to "invade" or use portions of the trust principal in order to support the beneficiary, but such power has to be exercised reasonably. Invasion of principal must be based on existing facts and reasonable future anticipations, with due regard for the purposes for which the power was given and also for the rights of those whose interests might be injured.[7]

Because discretionary powers are usually conferred in general terms, a trustee faces difficult individual decisions based on specific facts. A beneficiary may want trust money to buy a house, a yacht, or purchase a seat on the New York stock exchange. When deciding such requests, a trustee must always apply "reasonable judgment."

Frequency of Trust Payments

From a relatively superficial point of view, trust beneficiaries are possibly most concerned about when they will be paid. Obviously the abstract need to protect the trust corpus and guarantee continued healthy investment income are far more important, but definitely less tangible than a check to a potential recipient.

The settlor or testator creating a trust would do well to take care in setting out the trustee's specific powers and duties regarding frequency of payment to beneficiaries. Some trusts command payment at irregular intervals as trust income is earned, introducing a constant note of uncertainty. Other trust terms allow payment when a beneficiary makes a request, but this can cause repeated problems, especially if a recipient is improvident and demanding.

Based on experience, possibly the most workable arrangement is to give a trustee discretion to make extraordinary payments in an emergency, combined with payments at regular intervals, usually at least quarterly.

The settlor also must decide whether or not to allow beneficiaries to have access to the trust principal for payment. If invasion of principal is permitted, the issue is to what extent it is to be allowed. Obviously, a beneficiary with unrestricted power to invade principal possesses the power to terminate the trust at any time. If principal depletion is a real possibility, it is best to set a maximum annual percentage on principal withdrawal.

Care, Support and Maintenance

The largest part of a trustee's activity involves decisions and interpretations of trust intent. No area is more difficult than discretionary decisions concerning possible invasion of trust principal to provide "comfortable care, support, and maintenance" for a beneficiary.

Over the years thousands of court cases have addressed this problem of support and maintenance as beneficiaries have objected to trustee actions or refusals to act.

For example, in one actual case, a settlor specified in the trust declaration during their lives he and his wife were to receive principal payments for their "comfortable care, support, and maintenance."

Regarding his sister, he specified trust principal could be invaded to the extent the trustee deemed necessary for her "care and maintenance" but "support" was not mentioned. The trustee decided he was required to supply funds from principal for the sister's basic care and maintenance *only, but* not "obliged to see that she was comfortable or properly supported."

This narrow decision had these practical results: sister's monthly rent was paid, but $100 per month for an automobile was denied. Health insurance premiums were paid because "it would make good business sense to eliminate, conceivably, heavy expenses for the trust later on." Monthly payments of $25 for "personal care," including hairdressers' bills, $25 for church contributions and $35 for recreation were all denied.

In making his judgment, the trustee took into account the amount of income received by the sister from other sources. Court decisions whether and to what extent a trustee should consider a beneficiary's other resources in deciding whether to invade principal are highly inconsistent, usually turning on facts and judicial whim. Similar considerations govern trustee interpretations of the meaning of what is "reasonable," or "proper," or "adequate."

A trustee with discretionary power to invade principal for the beneficiary's support and maintenance must give precedence to the interests of the life tenant over those of the remainderman unless otherwise directed by the declaration. If there are two or more beneficiaries, the trustee must consider both equally.

A trustee cannot skimp on providing for a beneficiary. The practical limit on such support is the size of the trust corpus, not the alleged standard of living of a beneficiary or other subjective factors.

Trustees generally take great care in making discretionary payments of income out of trust principal because they are aware error in such cases may constitute a breach of trust, cause possible litigation and impose personal liability on them.

Corporate trustees often employ the device of advisory committee consideration of requests for discretionary payouts. In a bank trust department, for example, such a committee may include four or six officers assigned to the trust department. While the decision is still left to the sole trustee, it is made after a collective advisory judgement by an experienced group.

Beneficiary Rights and Duties

The trustee exists in order to promote the interests of the trust beneficiaries, all of whom he must treat with equality and impartiality. Even when exercising discretionary powers over distributions of trust income, the trustee cannot favor one over another.

The trustee must exercise scrupulous fairness toward a beneficiary, including providing full details of any particular trust matter when a reasonable request for such information is made. He must keep accounts revealing the nature, cost, and manner of administration of trust property, and these accounts must be rendered in full detail at reasonable intervals.

He must collect and distribute trust income to beneficiaries after making necessary deductions and allowances. Normally, income distributions are made on a regular basis and, unless the trust agreement specifies otherwise, without regard to the recipients' ability to manage or spend wisely.

Unlike the U.S., where a trust continues in existence until its express purposes are fulfilled, in England and many common law nations a trust can be terminated voluntarily by joint action of the beneficiaries under certain conditions.

In the trust declaration the settlor usually indicates the nature and extent of the beneficiary's interests and rights. A beneficiary has the right to expect a trustee's completely loyal administration of the trust corpus.

A beneficiary's property rights are full and unrestricted, unless the trust instrument provides for specific restrictions. Generally, the equitable title held by the beneficiary allows him to exercise his property rights as would the holder of the legal title, and courts will enforce these rights.

When there are two or more beneficiaries, each has equal rights and they hold the property as tenants in common. Where control of property is at issue, a majority of beneficiaries cannot in any way prejudice a minority or assume any greater rights. Each beneficiary can act independently of all others and cannot be hindered in such action by any other beneficiary.

A beneficiary's interest in trust property may be transferred voluntarily and legally, unless the trust declaration prohibits it. The law of the jurisdiction of the trust at times governs the transfer of a beneficiary's interest, as in the case of an "involuntary transfer" after a beneficiary dies intestate. Then the interest passes to statutory heirs in accordance with the state law on post mortem distribution of property.

Beneficiary Liabilities

Though we often hear that rights are accompanied by responsibilities, a beneficiary under a trust usually has only a general liability to the trust based on beneficial or equitable ownership of trust property.

A beneficiary has no obligation to reimburse a trustee for administrative expenses unless he or she agrees to do so. Nor can a trustee use trust property to satisfy personal debts a beneficiary owes a trustee.

If a beneficiary is allowed to borrow from the trust corpus, he or she is fully liable for repayment of the debt.[8] Where a beneficiary owes a personal debt to the settlor of the trust, the status as beneficiary does not absolve the debtor of repayment.[9] A beneficiary may incur liability by dealing wrongfully with trust property, and where a loss occurs as a result, it can be made up from the beneficiary's equitable interest in the trust property. The beneficiary may also be personally liable for repayment if he is overpaid by the trust, even if in error.

A beneficiary incurs personal liability as a result of a breach of trust by criminal participation or collusion with others against the trust. For example, when one of several beneficiaries improperly persuaded a trustee to loan funds without proper authorization, that beneficiary was held personally responsible to the co-beneficiaries. An offending beneficiary's portion of the trust estate can be subject to an equitable lien in favor of other beneficiaries.

Even when a beneficiary asserts undue pressure on a trustee, if he takes the desired action, it is the trustee who remains liable if he exceeds his authority. However, where beneficiaries actively interfered with a trustee's duties, they cannot later bring legal action against the trustee for any damage that results.

Limited Beneficiary Rights

Both the American "spendthrift trust" and the common law "protective trust" described earlier restrict the power of a beneficiary to act with regard to trust property, especially the right to transfer such property, including equitable ownership.

A settlor, in creating such a trust, has the right and power to restrict a beneficiary's right to alienate or transfer any interest in trust property. These restraints apply to assignment of trust income or trust principal, or both. In some few states the law forbids restraints on transfers of principal, and in a few jurisdictions, restraints on either income or principal are illegal in a trust declaration.

In most states the intention of the settlor takes precedence in creating restrictions in a spendthrift trust. Specific words are not required, and if the terms of the trust clearly indicate intended restraints on a beneficiary's power to transfer his interest in trust property, that intention will guide decisions of both the trustee and courts that may have jurisdiction.

Duration of a Trust

The trust, by its very nature, has as its general goal, successful long-term estate administration and management. Therefore one of the most important provisions in a trust declaration or agreement is that setting the period of time during which the trust is to operate.

We have already mentioned the ancient common law **rule against perpetuities**, that states a trust legally can exist only during the lifetimes of a reasonable number of persons ("all my children") who are alive at the time the trust is created, plus 21 years (meaning 21 years after the death of the last beneficiary to die). Some U.S. state statutes specify that only the lives of two named persons may be used as the gauge of duration. One state, Louisiana, limits trust existence to the lifetime of *only one* person.

As developed by the experience of the common law, rules regarding trust duration oppose the dead hand of the past forever restricting the future use of property, especially real estate. The common law believed in the principle of free alienability of property, and thus the purpose of limiting trust duration is to confine trust operation to a reasonable period of time during which a testator or settlor can realistically foresee the needs of the beneficiaries. This is true whether the trust objective is the care of children until they reach majority, or the support of a remaining spouse for the remainder of a lifetime.

The key question is not how long the trust legally can continue, but rather, in the interests of the beneficiaries, how long *should* it continue? For example, a family trust will have utility only so long as the family unit is likely to endure, then the trust corpus would be better sold and proceeds distributed to remaindermen. Some times "utility" means until the remaining spouse remarries or dies, or until all children leave the parental home and are on their own. It may be until the incompetent beneficiary of a trust dies, or until the last aged beneficiary passes away.

Shifting the burden of decision about duration of a trust to a trustee does not solve the problem, since a trustee faces the same difficult choices a testator or settlor faces. For that reason, experienced trustees wisely decline to accept responsibility for a trust giving them discretionary power to terminate the trust at some future date of their choosing.

Each trust creation case has different considerations and the only consistency is the fact that no testator or settlor can look into the future with certainty. No pat formula can cover all possible contingencies. The truth is, there is no ideal length of time during which a trust should remain in effect.

For these very real and practical reasons, the law sets the maximum limit for trust duration. Within the established common law and statutory limitations, most realistic trust objectives can be accommodated.

Trusts for Business and Investment

The Business Trust

As an historic preface to our discussion of the commercial role of trusts, consider a trust once popular in America, the so-called "business trust" or "Massachusetts trust," named after the state in which it first appeared in 1856. It is also called a "common law trust" because this trust does not depend on statutory authorization for its creation.

Although still used in jurisdictions that offer greater tax advantages for trusts compared to corporations, the original Massachusetts trust is said to have become popular because that state imposed certain statutory restrictions on corporations developing and dealing in real estate and also did not allow limited liability companies for certain business purposes.

This hybrid legal device is unique because it was designed to actively operate a business and produce profits, as compared to conventional trusts used simply for asset protection, tax avoidance and passive income production.

Part partnership, part corporation, the business trust is a voluntary association of trustees who actively hold title to property and operated a business under the terms of a joint trust agreement, for the benefit of shareholders who also own the trust and share in profits. When shareholders actually exercise control over the business, they and the trustees become personally liable for trust debts to the extent of their investment; conversely, shareholder trust interests can be attached by their personal creditors. Much like a limited partnership, if shareholders exercise no control over a business trust, they are personally exempt from creditor attack. Shareholder personal liability is the great disadvantage of the business trust.

This arrangement is somewhat like a corporation, but is easier to form, requiring no formal registration with the state *in most jurisdictions), only a signed agreement among the parties. Since this trust is entirely private, it can avoid many government reporting requirements and conceal actual owners. The business trust was often a means for interstate operations, avoiding business registration in other states as well as "blue sky" laws restricting the sale of out-of-state securities.

There are some asset protection possibilities in the business trust; consider a situation in which a business is run by a father, obviously exposed to personal liability for potential business claims or other litigation. His family's home, bank accounts and other assets could be deeded to a business trust in which he has no ownership, but is the managing trustee. This gives him 100 percent control of his business, and exempts the trust assets of the beneficial owners, his non-participatory wife and children, from business and personal creditor attack.

While the business trust arrangement has some limited potential value as an asset protection device, there are many other methods discussed here better suited to that role, without mixing asset protection with the unpredictability of an active business enterprise.

Reviewing the history and form of the Massachusetts trust simply confirms what the following pages demonstrate; trusts still have an important role to play in business, commerce and industry.

Trusts and Family Businesses

Whether a family business is a corporation, partnership, sole proprietorship or a limited liability company, the owners sooner or later must deal with the issue of future management and ownership.

Any prudent business owner will hesitate before giving stock to children, a spouse or trusted employees because of the real possibility that stock can be sold, encumbered or fall into the hands of hostile persons. Such eventualities are often avoided by a mutual shareholders' agreement that defines in writing permitted classes of shareholders or transferees, limiting stock transfers by gift, sale or testamentary disposition to those within the defined groups, usually lineal descendants of existing shareholders or other shareholders themselves.

In a case where a stock sale outside these groups is proposed, or upon the disability or retirement of a shareholder, these agreements will usually grant the right of first refusal, or "cross-purchase" as it is called, to the other shareholders on a pro rata basis, or to the corporation itself, called "redemption."

As you will see, properly crafted trusts can serve as a useful medium to retain control and pass future business ownership to a surviving spouse, heirs or trusted employees.

Investment Trusts

Long before the disastrous financial collapse of the South Seas Company in 1720, **investment trusts** for the general public were a well-known and accepted form of business trust in England and later in America. During the 19th century "industrial revolution" investment trusts returned and flourished. Today they play a highly important role in commercial investments and business.

Most of the discussion in this book has involved personal use of trust mechanisms to benefit one's self, your family and, in this chapter, as a means to assert and pass on family business control and ownership.

The investment trust moves the trust concept beyond the circle of self, family and personal business out into the wide world of public investment and finance. It offers the benefit of avoiding corporate income taxes, thereby increasing the potential for personal profit. It operates on the same general trust principles, although here the trustees function more as a board of directors, the trust conducts its affairs much as a corporation would, and the persons who voluntarily invest in the investment trust, the beneficiaries who receive trust income usually are known as "unitholders."

Investment trusts can be organized as limited partnerships or limited liability companies, with the articles of either serving as a trust instrument or declaration. Use of these forms can complicate trust operation because of the regulation state law imposes on such entities, but their virtue is in lower taxes compared to other businesses.

Investment trusts sells shares or "units" to the general public, much as shares are sold in a corporation, offering similar investment advantages of other publicly traded businesses. Pooling the assets of thousands of investors under a single unified management, trustees make hopefully wise investments that repay investors with lower tax income, increased value of units owned or in dividends paid.

Real Estate Investment Trusts (REITs):

As the name indicates, this trust specializes in real estate investments, its shares trade like common stock, and investors are able to make low-cost, high-yield investments. "High-yield" because U.S. tax law requires the REIT to pass on a full 95 percent of its net income to investors annually. This type of trust is primarily a domestic U.S. entity, although possibilities exist for structuring such trusts in other countries.

REITs come in several combination forms, including mortgage REITs, or specialize in certain types of real estate including shopping centers, apartments, and health care facilities like nursing homes.

REITs in the U.S. also have the tax advantage of "pass through" to shareholders of deductions for interest and depreciation, thus are partially tax sheltered. When finally REIT shares are taxed, it is likely to be at a long-term capital gains tax rate of 28 percent, rather than a possible 39.6 percent top income tax rate, another plus.

REITs can be owned by both foreign and domestic pension funds, but in order to discourage rich investors from transferring real estate from corporation to REITs, no fewer than five individuals can own more than 50 percent of any REIT's total shares.

Royalty investment trusts:

This REIT invests in oil, gas or other mineral companies that assign their royalty rights to the trust, which in turns sells individual units to investors. Unitholders are entitled to "royalties," meaning energy sale proceeds less all production costs. Favorable oil depletion allowances and other business deductions flow through to the investor since there is no trust income tax. In high energy price periods this arrangement produces very high levels of income, at least until the oil and gas runs out, leaving no return on principal. But oil and gas is a "boom or bust" type of business and royalty investment trusts follow the same risky path.

Unit investment trusts:

Often called "unit investment trusts," under this arrangement trust managers buy securities, usually tax-exempt bonds, with funds from the initial offering and hold them for long-term investment return until maturity. This allows low-cost management, but the return to the investor is directly tied to the general state of the bond market at the time of purchase, thus limiting possible investment return in periods of down turn.

Miscellaneous investment trusts:

While these trusts are not generally of importance as individual investment vehicles, several types of trusts have great economic clout in the investment world because of the aggregate amount of money they wield on behalf of others. These include employee pension and profit-sharing plans, trust mechanisms tightly regulated by federal law in order to protect their beneficiaries, financed by employer and employee contributions. Other trusts of a similar nature include stock ownerships trusts created to distribute shares to qualified employees, or stock bonus trusts with a similar goal.

Somewhat akin to these investment trusts are private trusts for individual retirement funds. In the U.S. these include such trusts as Keogh plans, 401K plans and individual retirement accounts (IRAs).

Offshore Trusts

The Offshore Asset Protection Trust

In recent years an asset protection device in trust form has gained wide popularity amongst a select few who are "in the know."

The offshore **asset protection trust** ("**APT**") is a personal trust created and based in a foreign nation which, when properly arranged, can be very advantageous to people seeking protection for their assets. This trust acts as a shield for business and personal assets against demanding creditors, protracted litigation and other potentially unpleasant financial liabilities, maybe even an ex-spouse bent on revenge.

In APT creation one central fact must be fully understood and accepted -- this trust arrangement will succeed only if planned and created in prospective, at a time of personal financial calm. It is unlikely to succeed if attempted in response to a pending personal financial crisis, and taking such a step under creditor pressure not only compounds problems, it can incur criminal liability.

If a foreign trust is hastily established when one is about to be, or has been sued or forced into personal bankruptcy, the act of transferring assets is likely to violate strict American civil and criminal "fraudulent conveyance" laws designed to protect creditors. These laws allow a court to declare a trust, or any similar device used to conceal or remove assets from creditors, null and void. The establishment of the trust near in time to filing or after bankruptcy is filed, or after litigation begins also is strong evidence of fraud, a crime in itself.

As a practical matter, regardless of when a foreign APT is created, any assets physically remaining within an American court's jurisdiction are not usually protected from judgement creditors simply because title to the property has been placed in the name of a foreign trustee. If tangible assets actually have been transferred to the foreign jurisdiction, as in the case of funds moved to an offshore bank account, a creditor definitely will have great difficulty in reaching them, provided he can even find out the account exists.

In litigation-crazed America, the sensible business or professional person does not wait for the day of disaster to begin planning asset protection. Medical, legal and professional malpractice suits, as well as legislative and judicial imposition of no-fault personal liability on corporate officers and directors are all now sad facts of business life. An active business or professional person can suddenly be held personally responsible for a corporation's alleged environmental pollution, a bank failure, or simply a dissatisfied employee or client who sues. Proof of the seriousness of the current situation is underscored by the huge premiums demanded for all types of malpractice insurance coverage. In this climate astute people must consider and adopt the best means available to protect their personal assets.

The best way to achieve a litigation-proof status is to minimize the chance of losing assets, and that is accomplished by shrinking the target. A smaller target is created by relinquishing legal title and control over assets, at least on paper. The APT is one of the legal devices that can accomplish that goal quickly and efficiently.

Up Front Costs

In addition to timing, there is another important factor to consider before creating an offshore trust.

Because the trust situs will be in a foreign jurisdiction, the cost of creating an average asset protection trust abroad usually exceeds U.S.$15,000 initially, plus several thousand dollars in annual maintenance fees. As a practical matter, unless the total assets to be shielded are worth more than $2 million, a foreign APT may not be practical because of creation costs.

Where To Establish an APT

Several offshore financial centers now exist in nations that tailor their statutory law to be hospitable to foreign-owned asset protection trusts. What the State of Delaware is to corporations in America, these nations are to asset protection trusts. Although these "nations" may be diminutive in geographic size and total population, their capital cities have well-developed, efficient banking and legal communities who understand APT law and finance.

Among the established APT havens are the Caribbean area nations of the Cayman Islands, the Bahamas, St. Kitts and Nevis, the British Virgin Islands, Belize, and the Turks and Caicos Islands; in the south Pacific, the Cook Islands, associated with nearby New Zealand; the British-associated Isle of Man, between Britain and Ireland; and Cyprus and Gibraltar, at either end of the Mediterranean.

If you are considering a personal foreign asset protection trust, check out one of these prospective foreign jurisdiction. Become familiar with local laws to assure yourself the legal and financial situation is favorable and offers the shelter you seek. Examine the recent record of economic and political stability, the reputation of lawyers and the judicial system, local taxes, the general business climate, possible language barriers, and the state of available communications and financial facilities.

These days with near-instant international bank transfers, telephones and faxes, most areas of the world have few problems providing the kind of communication services an APT and its creator needs. It is really no more difficult than dealing with a local bank in your home area, although phone bills do mirror the actual distance.

A foreign APT trustee can even pay your mortgage payments and other personal bills on a regular basis, as your needs require.

Strong Creditor Deterrent

Given the need for protection and proper initial timing, even with the potential cost, you still can use an APT to counter most threats to your hard-earned assets, placing them safely beyond the reach of potential domestic litigation plaintiffs, creditors and contingent fee lawyers. While the APT concept may be novel in your experience, many thousands of American citizens have successfully followed this international road to wealth protection.

Here are some of the features that make an APT so attractive:

- The courts of the foreign jurisdictions mentioned usually do not honor or even recognize the validity of non-domestic court orders. In any of these nations, a foreign creditor bent upon collection will be forced to re-litigate completely in a local court, after hiring local lawyers, the original claim that gave rise to the foreign judgment. The sheer legal complexity and cost of such an international collection effort is likely to stop all but the most determined adversaries.
- An offshore asset protection trust can consist of little more than a trust account in a local bank in the foreign country. Respected multi-national banks can provide trustees and staff experienced in trust matters. With today's instant communications and international banking, it is as convenient to hold assets and accounts overseas as it is locally.
- In the countries named, a settlor of a foreign asset protection trust has the right to exercise far greater control over trust assets and income than permitted under

domestic trust law in countries that are not catering to APT business. Rules that frown on the creation of a trust by a settlor for his or her own benefit do not apply in these countries. In most jursidictions not in the APT business, a trust created by a settlor in which the settlor is also the beneficiary is void as to the settlor's creditors. This rule does not apply in these foreign jurisdictions seeking APT business.
- Domestic creditors faced with the costly tangle of enforcing a judgment in a foreign country are likely to be discouraged, if not completely dissuaded. More importantly, the foreign law usually does not support strict application of American (or other) fraudulent conveyance law. In some of these countries the strict statute of limitations imposed on a creditor's suit is two years from the date on which the APT was established. In others, like the Cook Islands, the limit is one year. It may take a creditor longer than that just to discover the existence of a foreign APT.
- An offshore APT is an excellent device to achieve international diversification of investments; your foreign trustee handles the investments and paper work, while you give long-distance advice and suggestions. In this way, you can take advantage of the world's best investment opportunities, without worrying about national borders or conflicting laws.
- The APT can provide privacy, confidentiality, and reduced domestic reporting requirements, avoid domestic taxes and probate in case of death, increase flexibility in conducting affairs in case of personal disability, in transferring assets, or avoiding domestic currency controls. Of course, an APT is a good substitute for, or supplement to, costly professional liability insurance or even a prenuptial agreement, offering strong protection of assets for heirs and their inheritance.

Creating an APT

Unfortunately, there are a limited number of qualified experts in the field of asset protection law, so proceed with great caution before choosing your personal advisor for such an important project. This is not an area of activity in which to cut corners. Knowledgeable APT attorneys and financial advisors tend to be expensive, but well worth the price.

The legal structure of a foreign asset protection trust differs little from that of an ordinary trust. The **settlor** creates the asset protection trust, transferring title to assets to the APT, to be administered according to the trust declaration by a managing **trustee** for named **beneficiaries**. Usually foreign law requires the naming of three trustees (the settlor usually may not serve), two located in the settlor's country of origin, and one independent managing trustee located in the foreign country.

Foreign trust law, unlike strict American "arm's length" requirements, allows a non-national settlor to receive income and benefits from the trust, while also maintaining effective control over the investment and distribution of the trust principal.

The trust **declaration** can give the settlor a large measure of control, including the right to replace the foreign trustee at any time with another nominee, and the right of prior approval of investments or distributions. Beneficiaries can vary according to the settlor's estate planning objectives, and the settlor may be a beneficiary.

Many foreign jurisdictions also require appointment of a local "**trust protector**" who, as the title indicates, is a neutral party who generally oversees the operation of the trust to insure its objectives are met and the law is followed. A protector does not manage the trust, but can veto trustee actions in some cases.

In most of these countries very little information about an APT must be registered with the government. The terms of the trust agreement and the parties involved need not be disclosed, and any information filed is not available as part of a public record. The only public record is a registry of APTs by name, date of creation and the name of the local trustee. In these privacy-conscious countries, a trustee is allowed to reveal information only in very limited circumstances, and then usually only by local court order.

The one feature of a foreign asset protection trust that worries most people is the distance between them and their assets, or at least the people who manage those assets. Naturally there is a justified concern about choosing reliable people to create and assist in managing your trust. As we said, in each of the countries mentioned the legal and banking community has extensive experience creating and managing APTs. Nevertheless, this is definitely a situation where references are in order, and each one should be checked carefully before a decision is made.

Operating a Foreign APT

While assets need not be transferred physically to the foreign country where the trust exists, circumstances may dictate such a precautionary move. Generally it is advisable to transfer cash and intangible assets such as stocks, bonds, and securities to a foreign trust. Easily portable assets, such as precious metal coins, jewelry or gem stones also can be transferred.

Simply transferring title to real estate or a business located in your home country to a foreign trust is questionable because the assets themselves remain within easy reach of creditors and courts. For other reasons we have already warned against an attempted transfer of property to an APT at a time of personal financial crisis, but in theory such a move may bring the APT within the putative jurisdiction of your home country court, if a judge uses the transfer to justify a finding the APT is doing business in your country. Such a judicial finding is not guaranteed to have any meaningful impact on the APT itself, however, since it is not binding on a foreign court.

One thing is certain: the foreign managing APT trustee should have no U.S. connections that might subject him or her to direct or indirect pressure from U.S. courts. If an international bank trust department is being considered as your foreign trustee, ask them bluntly what their policy is in such situations. It would probably be better to go with Barclays as trustee, than Chase Manhattan's local foreign branch.

APT Combined With a Limited Partnership

There is wisdom in the advice that some asset protection lawyers suggest: combine the APT with a family limited partnership.

In this arrangement husband and wife might control 5 percent as managing general partners, title to the other 95 percent of the assets in the partnership could be transferred to your children as limited partners. If they are Americans, gift taxes can be avoided up to $20,000 annually for both spouses' transfers into the partnership and part of the $1.2 million estate tax exemption can be used as well. This also reduces eventual estate taxes, if any.

This may sound like a drastic surrender of your wealth to your children, but it really is not. In a limited partnership the limited partners, the children, have no control at all over the assets. The 5 percent managing general partners, you and your spouse, have all the control. You decide cash distributions, what salary you are to be paid as managers, what investments are to be made. Although the limited partners own the assets, the are inactive owners forbidden by law to control those assets lest they jeopardize their partnership status and their limited liability.

An extra tough layer of asset protection is achieved when the 95 percent limited partnership interest is transferred to an offshore asset protection trust you have created. That kind of legal distancing will certainly make potential creditors think twice before what can be highly complex and expensive litigation.

Creation of both a family limited partnership and a foreign asset protection trust can be made a package deal for about $15,000 to $20,000 by a good specialist law firm that "knows the ropes."

U.S. Tax Consequences for our American Readers

Under American tax law, foreign asset protection trusts as such are tax-neutral, as are domestic trusts, meaning trust income is treated as the settlor's reportable annual personal income, and taxed accordingly at personal income tax rates.

Because the settlor retains some degree of control over the transferred assets titled to a foreign APT, U.S. gift taxes on the transfer of assets can be avoided. At death, estate taxes are imposed on the value of trust assets for the settlor's estate, but all exemptions, such as $600,000 for martial assets can be used. Asset protection trusts also are usually not subject to the 35 percent U.S. excise tax imposed on transfers of property to a "foreign person," a point explored more fully below.

American law imposes on a settlor or beneficiary of any trust, including a foreign APT, the legal duty to disclose the existence of the trust on your federal tax returns, documents supposedly kept "confidential" by the IRS. In theory, creditors must obtain a court to order to gain access to your tax returns, and that takes time and expense.

Avoiding Income Tax on APT Income

Since 1966 when the current IRS rules were imposed, a trust settlor whose trust meets the four conditions stated in section 679 of the Internal Revenue Code is taxed annually on all income and gains earned by the trust, even if they are undistributed. In other words, all income earned by the trust is included in the settlor's U.S. gross personal income and taxed as such.

If your APT objectives are mainly for asset protection, privacy, or international diversification, this personal tax consequences will not matter a great deal.

However, if you plan is to use an APT for investment purposes, hopefully with positive trust income on a continuing basis, you should be aware of these four factors that make a settlor of an offshore trust personally liable for taxes on trust income.

This taxable status occurs when: 1) a "U.S. person" transfers assets, including cash, to a foreign trust; 2) the transfer is either direct or indirect; 3) the trust has one or more U.S. beneficiaries; and, 4) the trust is organized and located in a foreign country. Elimination of any one of these factors allows an American settlor to escape U.S. income taxes on the trust income.

The easiest criteria to change and thus avoid the tax is to have the offshore trust established by someone other than "a U.S. person," a phrase broadly defined by the tax code to include a U.S. citizen, resident alien, partnership, corporation, estate, or trust.

To qualify, the settlor of the foreign trust must be a foreigner, and this can be accomplished by having a foreign corporation establish the foreign trust. In order to maximize American tax benefits, the true settlor can form a foreign corporation, then transfer his U.S. assets to that corporation. Then the corporation, as settlor, forms a foreign trust, transferring its corporate assets to the new APT. Sounds complicated but it is only legal paperwork.

Offshore Trusts

The beneficiary of the foreign trust can be a U.S. citizen or resident, usually the true settlor's spouse, child or grandchild. The foreign corporation, as trust settlor, retains the power to change the beneficiary, revoke the trust, and control disposition of trust property. Of course, the settlor controls the corporation.

Under these circumstances, the trust and all its assets are located outside the United States, the corporate settlor is also foreign and has no obligation to file a U.S. tax return. If the trust is located in a tax haven country, there may be no tax imposed at all. The American beneficiaries are not subject to U.S. income taxes on income received from the trust, because the corporate settlor is the owner of the APT and as such, is responsible for trust income taxes, if any, only in the foreign nation in which incorporation occurred.

There is another way to avoid being taxed on the income earned by an offshore trust.

Since one of the IRS requirements for imposition of personal income tax is that the trust have a "U.S. person" as beneficiary, if there is no U.S. beneficiary, the settlor is not personally taxed on trust income he or she may receive. Simply set up the trust to benefit an entity not a "U.S. person," such as an offshore corporation as the beneficiary of the APT. Under the U.S. tax code, an offshore corporation is not considered a U.S. beneficiary of a foreign trust unless 50 percent or more of the corporation's voting power is controlled by "U.S. persons." So if a "U.S. person" is one of several persons you want to benefit from the trust, you can have these beneficiaries form an offshore corporation, taking care that they not own more than 50 percent of the voting stock.

If these conditions are met, an APT settlor in fact, will escape the IRS offshore trust income tax rules and no taxed is imposed on the trust income. The trust income can remain in the foreign trust undistributed and continue to compound and accumulate tax-free.

There is another method to avoid U.S. taxes on income from a foreign trust, but the settlor will not be around to enjoy this tax avoidance. IRS offshore trust income tax rules do not apply to a foreign testamentary trust created under a will. Neither the decedent's estate nor any "U.S. person" named as beneficiary of the trust can then be taxed on trust income.

This testamentary loophole allows income to accumulate tax-free in the foreign trust and to be invested anywhere in the world, including the United States, paying little or no taxes, depending on where the investments are made and how they are structured. If heirs do not need the income or assets of a decedent's estate immediately, a foreign testamentary trust following sound investment policies eventually can increase the inheritance many times over.

A Note of Caution

As we go to press the U.S. Department of the Treasury has asked Congress to change the rules concerning foreign trust income we have described. One proposal would impose full reporting requirements of all assets transferred to foreign trusts, with tough penalties for those who fail to report. The suggested changes will also require personal income taxes to be paid on any foreign trust income received, even if the recipient does not own the trust personally. The IRS wants these rule changes to take effect retroactively to February 6, 1995, the date on which they were made public.

What chance exists these new foreign trust income rules will be enacted is unknown, but in the context of demands for a balanced federal budget you should know these proposed rule changes could net the federal government an estimated $2.4 billion over a projected six-year period.

Obviously, you should keep up to date on any current developments concerning these proposals if you are interested in establishing a foreign APT.

Avoiding U.S. Excise Tax on Foreign Transfers

In transferring assets to a foreign asset protection trust, there is one more tax hurdle; the U.S. excise tax imposed on some transfers of property to foreign entities. The tax is imposed by section 1491 of the IRC, with exceptions stated in section 1492, on transfers by a "U.S. person" or entity to a foreign corporation, partnership, estate, trust, or partnership. A 35 percent tax is imposed on any appreciation in value of the transferred property from its original basis not otherwise recognized in the transfer. In other words, if you transfer appreciated property to a foreign trust, the transfer is taxable and you must pay either the regular capital-gains tax, or the 35 percent excise tax.

The easy way to avoid the 35 percent excise tax is to transfer cash or non-appreciated property to the foreign trust.

Foreign or "Offshore" Corporations

As we have mentioned. an offshore asset protection trust can be used in conjunction with an offshore corporation.

Some investment experts claim the perfect repository for asset protection is a corporation chartered in a foreign nation (an "offshore corporation") -- which you, as the instigator, will control through indirect means.

Theoretically, your foreign corporate ownership will be concealed from your government, allowing financial privacy while the corporation invests in foreign mutual funds or other valuable assets located outside your home country, thus sheltering income and profits from domestic taxes. Company business can theoretically be conducted through a designated nominee, further shielding your secret participation from creditors or the tax collector.

In theory this sounds grand, but there are many practical problems associated with an offshore corporation, not the least of which for Americans is compliance with U.S. law and penalties for failure to do so. Many other countries are now imposing similar restrictions on their citizens. What starts in the U.S. often gets adopted by other governments within a few years.

Firstly, just as in establishing any domestic corporation, legal formalities must be strictly followed when incorporating abroad, and the costs of setting up and maintaining a foreign company can be considerable. You need experienced local in-country legal counsel who understands your asset protection objectives. Corporations anywhere are rule-bound creatures requiring separate books and records, meetings, minutes and authorizing resolutions, all making it less flexible than other arrangements.

There are separate U.S. taxes on unrealized gains, on income from, and on capital gains accrued on property transferred to, a foreign corporation. If the offshore company can be characterized as a "foreign personal holding company" as defined by the IRS, an American shareholder's portion of undistributed earnings will be taxed currently to him as ordinary income each year. The same IRS rules apply if the offshore entity qualifies as a "controlled foreign corporation," but in that case, additional taxes are imposed on any gain derived from the sale of the corporate assets.

There are many problem U.S. court decisions strictly interpreting the obligations of a "U.S. person" actively involved in a foreign corporation. For those who seek the quiet secrecy a foreign corporation allegedly offers, these cases have pierced the offshore corporate vale, attributing "constructive ownership" to the involved U.S. taxpayer as an individual or finding actual control based on a "chain of entities" linking the U.S. taxpayer to the offshore corporation. American courts consistently identify the person with substantive control, as compared to paper nominees exercising nominal control.

Equally as serious, there are many specific IRS reporting requirements imposed on U.S. taxpayers involved in the creation of, or service as officer, director or 10 percent or greater shareholder of, a foreign personal holding company or offshore corporation.

The U.S. Supreme Court has ruled a U.S. taxpayer can be guilty of the crime of "falsifying a federal income tax return" by failing to report foreign corporate holdings and, further, that Fourth Amendment guarantees against unreasonable searches and seizures do not apply to documents located abroad pertaining to a U.S. taxpayer's ownership of foreign financial interests. These court holdings are underscored by many existing U.S.-foreign bilateral agreements allowing the surrender of documents in criminal tax investigations. When American courts conclude offshore corporations are used to conceal assets or avoid taxes, they levy added dollar penalties plus interest, and can impose criminal convictions as well.

This is not to say foreign corporations have no place in asset protection planning, but U.S. taxpayers should have no illusions about the legal and tax limitations which apply to them if they are involved as incorporators, officers, directors, shareholders -- or simply as beneficiaries of corporate acts.

This summary is only a brief introduction to the use and features of foreign trusts.

In Summary: Foreign asset protection trusts definitely can be extremely flexible financial and tax-planning devices. Though federal government efforts continue to eliminate these trust tax benefits, opportunities still remain. Remember offshore trust strategies are complicated and full of pitfalls, so when you venture abroad financially, go armed with the expert assistance of an experienced international tax and legal adviser -- whose only loyalty is to you.

Transfers of Property: Is It A Fraud?

In the previous chapter we discussed, as an integral part of your financial planning, the ways and means legally available to use an offshore asset protection trust. The objective is placing your property beyond the reach of others as securely as the law allows, while permitting you to retain, if not the title, at least a degree of control and influence over that property and its income.

We assume that when you adopt this legal means of asset protection, your intention is just that - to protect your property from unforeseen depredations, to make certain a secure economic future for you and your family.

But consider the view from the other side of the table, where your judgment creditor sits. What he or she sees is a person claiming to be "judgment proof," holding no personal title to property which can satisfy a just debt or judgment, and yet a person who appears to live a comfortable life of wealth and ease. Understandably your creditor, and ultimately the court he invokes in aid of his appeal, will want to know: "Where are the assets?"

The clear implication in that question is that you may have intentionally placed your assets in a sheltered position where they continue to benefit you, but where creditors cannot get to them - in other words, that you have defrauded your creditors by concealing or transferring away your assets.

An act which to you was simply good business judgment, now blossoms into allegations of fraud, with potential civil and criminal significance.

It is within this framework which we turn to a discussion of the law of fraudulent conveyances.

The Law of Fraudulent Conveyances:

The word "conveyance" is nothing more than the lawyer's description of the act of transferring legal title to property from one person to another. We all understand the meaning of fraud. Put them together and we have the act of transferring title to property in order to deceive, cheat or deprive someone of their legal right to that property.

Human nature being what it is, the problem of fraudulent conveyances is hardly something new. It was formally dealt with in statutory form by the English for the first time in the "Statute of Elizabeth" in 1570. The basic elements of the law have changed little since.

In its essentials the law states that any transfer of property made with the intent to hinder, delay or defraud creditors, is voidable by those creditors at their option, even though the transfer may remain valid as between the transferor and a "good faith" transferee.

In the United States the law of fraudulent conveyances has been formalized in the Uniform Fraudulent Conveyances Act (UFCA) and the Uniform Fraudulent Transfers Act (UFTA), each of which has been adopted as law by about half of the states.

The classic example of such chicanery would be the debtor who deliberately sells property, then hides the proceeds of the sale in a Swiss bank account, hoping to enjoy the money at some future time, meanwhile his just debts go unpaid.

As you might imagine, in real life fraudulent conveyances are rarely so blatant, but are far more subtle and sophisticated - like transferring property and assets to a foreign asset protection trust or offshore corporation, a limited partnership or a spouse's living trust.

That litany of asset protection devices should give you more than a hint - you too could face creditor charges of fraud, regardless of what your actual intent may have been at the time you transferred title to your assets to a seemingly impregnable asset protection device.

Any of these innocent-appearing actions can be alleged to fall within the definition of a "phony transfer," defined by Justice Brandeis of the U.S. Supreme Court in 1925 as a "transfer in trust" which in effect is "a transfer with absolute dominion reserved" by the transferor. In such a transfer, nothing changes realistically - the debtor signs over the title to some other entity, but continues the use and enjoyment of the property, be it "his" business, mansion or luxury yacht.

The late and notorious New York lawyer and social lion, Roy Cohn, for example, conducted business from a well-appointed law office, lived in a luxury West Side town house, had a yacht moored in the Hudson River, weekended at a country place in Greenwich, travelled elegantly in limousines and jetted around the world - yet owed millions of dollars to creditors, including the IRS - and had absolutely no property titled in his name. His estate (what little there is of it) and his law firm (which the IRS has attached), is still embroiled in court battles - and will be for years to come.

Intentional Fraud

The law of fraudulent conveyances requires as an essential element of proof, the showing of the **subjective fraudulent intent** of the transferor - a very difficult burden for a creditor, were it not for the development of a legal doctrine the courts have come to call "**badges of fraud.**"

Obviously, no court has yet figured out a way in which to inspect the contents of the human mind of a person charged with fraud so as to ascertain without question, what his or her intent may have been at the time of a transfer of assets. But since the time of Queen Elizabeth I and the original statute, courts have looked to certain evidences or marks of fraud, actions indicating true intention, the so-called "badges of fraud." These include conveyances in secret, conveyances made while creditor litigation is pending, or conveyances after which the debtor retains possession and use of the property "transferred." Without regard to actual intent, a court may find **constructive fraud**, as when a conveyance has the result of preventing the debtor from paying his debts, forcing him into insolvency, or of removing sufficient capital to operate his business as debts come due.

There are other indicators of fraud; simply giving away property to a friend, a spouse or child at a time when the debtor is in precarious financial condition; selling property for less than the true market value; the mere act of conveying away all of the debtor's assets at once, leaving him with little or nothing in his name.

The logical test in all these cases, as the law sees it, is to ask objectively whether the conduct of the debtor is that of a person who is trying to cheat his creditors.

Creditors' Remedies

The importance of the answer to that question lies in the fact that a court can, and will, overturn a transfer of property if the answer is "yes." Depending upon the jurisdiction, the creditor has from two to six years under the statute of limitations to seek action, although under U.S. federal bankruptcy law, it is one year.

When a creditor can show these badges of fraud, or evidence of constructive fraud, the burden of proof shifts to the debtor, who then must show he or she had no such fraudulent intent.

And there is an important point to consider; the debt may have been incurred prior to the transfer of assets, or the debt may have been incurred even after the transfer of assets - a time sequence having significance for those who thought their assets were secure because of their prior planning.

Using Offshore Trusts, Annuities, and Portfolio Bonds

The creditor may be able to convince a court to issue a restraining order or an injunction against a pending transfer of assets; to appoint a conservator who takes control of the debtor's property; or allow a judgment creditor to void the transfer, and directly to attach the property after it has been transferred, regardless of who or what holds title to it.

If the property subject to such an order is within the court's legal jurisdiction, any designs one may have had for "asset protection" disappear when the marshals or sheriffs arrive with the writs.

In Summary: Now that you understand the law of fraudulent conveyances, you can easily accept why its potential application to any of your proposed property transfers must be carefully considered. You can also appreciate why asset protection planning must be done, and plans executed, well in advance of any possible financial trouble - not when the proverbial wolf is at the door.

Offshore Trusts

Swiss Annuities As Alternatives To Trusts

Most people think of annuities as simply investment vehicles. When the topic becomes Swiss annuities, however, these investments take on an added dimension of safety. What most people don't realize is that Swiss annuities, along with their competitive rates, steady dividends, and security, offer another important benefit -- that of asset protection.

In recent years a great many people, including professionals, directors of companies, and investors (both large and small), have become increasingly concerned about protecting their assets from liability claims and creditors. In the past, those concerned with protecting their wealth would often set up trusts. Indeed, in response to this growing need, several offshore companies have begun offering trusts that are designed specifically to protect one's assets from creditors. Largely lost amid the hype and various types of investments being offered are Swiss annuities.

Swiss annuities are products of the Swiss insurance industry. This alone sets them apart from other investment options, because the integrity of the Swiss insurance industry is protected by Swiss law. Insurance products, including annuities, enjoy that protection in a rather unique, but extremely solid manner.

In general legal proceedings, creditors are permitted to seize insurance policies, bought by debtors, to pay off money owed during a collection procedure against the debtor. Creditors may also have insurance policies included in a debtor's estate in a bankruptcy proceeding. This type of legal proceeding is also usually true of Swiss law (according to Article 79, Paragraph 1 of the Swiss Insurance Act), provided that the policy owner has designated a third part as the beneficiary of the policy. The designation of the beneficiary is voided if the insured individual declares bankruptcy or if his or her creditors seize the policy.

However, if the policy owner of the Swiss insurance policy, or annuity, has *irrevocably* designated a third party as his or her beneficiary, or if the owner of the policy has *irrevocably or revocably* designated his or her spouse and/or descendants as beneficiaries of the policy, the policy is protected from the policy owner's creditors (Article 80, Swiss Insurance Act).

At first glance when considering using a Swiss annuity or insurance policy for asset protection, one might think that the policy owner must relinquish control over his or her assets to protect them. However, at closer inspection, it becomes clear that this is an excellent method for securing protection. By revocably designating a spouse and/or descendants as beneficiaries, the assets are protected from creditors. The key word of course is *revocable*. The owner not only gains protection, but he or she retains control of the annuity. As time goes by, and the conditions and demands of life change, the owner of the policy may review his or her financial situation and decide to revoke the designation of beneficiaries. Obviously, depending on circumstances, policy owners may simply leave the designated beneficiaries as they are, may decide to buy more annuities, or extend the terms of existing ones. Unquestionably, the policy owner enjoys a large measure of flexibility with asset management.

Swiss Annuities and Asset Protection

One of the most vital areas of the Swiss financial markets is the insurance industry. While Swiss banks are associated with safety and conservative management, the insurance industry has not had a single company failure in more than 130 years. This is a record that surpasses even the steadiness of Swiss banks.

About twenty insurance companies compete in Switzerland. All are financially sound and managed with an eye for safety and high return. Usually, the two conditions -- safety and high yield regarding investments -- are mutually exclusive. High yield implies risk. Unlike the insurance industries in other countries, however, insurance companies in Switzerland enjoy unique tax advantages. Coupled with efficient and intelligent management, Swiss insurance companies are able to offer a variety of steady and productive investment opportunities.

Of all the investment options offered by Swiss insurance companies, annuities provide excellent benefits and can be used for asset protection. The typical annuity is an investment that enables the investor to place money in a tax-advantaged plan. A common purpose of many annuities is to set aside money for retirement. A major benefit of annuities is that they allow investors to defer taxes on savings. Thus, the investor is able to build assets more quickly than can be done with other, often more risky, investments. Annuities can be used to save money for a variety of purposes, however, they are most frequently used as retirement accounts. For the individual concerned with asset protection, annuities provide a means of achieving solid returns while deferring taxes.

Annuities, especially Swiss annuities with the added features of their strength and potential for asset protection, possess many prominent advantages:

- Annuities can be structured so that there is no investment ceiling. The annuity owner can contribute as much as he or she wants each year.
- Because annuities provide tax-deferment, the money in the account grows faster than other investments with similar rates of return. Furthermore, many investors wait to take money out of annuities after they have retired and are in a lower tax bracket. In this way they pay less taxes and save more of their money.

- Annuities offer superior security for the investor's family. Should the investor die before the earnings of the annuity are distributed, beneficiaries can receive the full value of the annuity.
- Record-keeping for annuities is simple. Because taxes are deferred, it is not necessary to file forms regarding annuities with the IRS until payments begin.
- Asset protection via Swiss annuities is much cheaper than asset protection through many other investments, particularly trusts. Establishing a trust, and then paying for management of it, can require rather hefty fees. Any fees through Swiss annuities are minor, and asset protection carries no extra cost at all. It is a standard feature of any Swiss annuity or insurance policy.
- Annuities are flexible investment options. Beneficiaries, for example, may be changed depending upon changing personal situations. In the case of divorce the annuity owner may wish to remove his or her former spouse from the annuity as beneficiary.

The Many Added Advantages of Swiss Annuities

Swiss annuities offer many advantages over annuities offered in other countries. Annuities have, in fact, been offered since the early 1970s, however, the financial markets have seen truly impressive growth in the area of annuities during the last few years. In the United States alone, the sales of annuities run close to $50 billion every year.

Despite their growing popularity, many people remain confused about annuities. Some think of them as being much the same as a mutual fund. While annuities can offer similar rates of returns, they have a major advantage -- annuities defer taxes until retirement. Mutual funds do not. Further, annuities can be set up in a way that once the investor begins to draw on the funds, he or she will receive regular payments for life.

The costs for annuities are also different than the costs for mutual funds. Because annuities are offered by insurance companies, for most annuities, the investor does not have to pay any commissions or front-end load fees. In most cases, there are penalties for withdrawing funds early, but these usually apply only for the first few years after an annuity has been opened. Swiss annuities, however, limit any "surrender" fees to the first year. This is a major consideration and advantage for investors in purchasing Swiss annuities over the annuities sold elsewhere.

Swiss annuities offer even more benefits. In many countries where annuities are offered, including the U.S., annuities are loosely regulated in comparison to other types of investments. In Switzerland, annuities are closely regulated, reducing risks to investors. Unlike the annuities sold in the U.S., which are backed by the dollar, which has been eroding steadily in value and purchasing power throughout the last hundred years, Swiss annuities are backed by the Swiss franc. The Swiss franc is far more stable, because it is backed by gold.

The payout plan for Swiss annuities is flexible and the payout is guaranteed. Indeed, payments can be set up to meet the individual needs of each investor. Payments can be sent out on annual, semi-annual, or quarterly schedules (a monthly schedule is available to Swiss residents). Although payments are denominated in Swiss francs, investors may instruct the insurance company to convert the payment into any currency they wish. Of course, they may make the conversions themselves at their bank in Switzerland. The Swiss insurance company will gladly send the payment to the investor, wherever he or she lives, or to the investor's bank.

In regards to taxes, Swiss annuities are also very attractive investments. Swiss annuities are exempt from the 35% withholding tax that foreigners who hold Swiss bank accounts must pay on their interest. Perhaps more importantly, investors do not have to report

Swiss annuities to either Swiss or U.S. tax agencies, although U.S. buyers of Swiss annuities must pay a 1% federal excise tax on the purchase of the policy. IRS Form 720 requires only that a calculation for an excise tax of 1% be made for the purchase of any foreign policy, however, no details of the policy need be reported. The excise tax payment is required to be paid only once at the time of the purchase of the policy. It is the investor's responsibility to report it. Swiss insurance companies do not provide any information regarding the purchase of annuities, the amount or number of payments made into the policy, or any earnings to government agencies in the U.S. or Switzerland. Confidentiality is assured.

Along with all this, Swiss annuities provide asset protection at no additional cost. In many cases, policies can be designed to afford protection from the beneficiary's creditors as well as the creditors of the annuity owner. If the annuity is structured so that payments are provided for the beneficiary, but the beneficiary has not made any contributions to the purchase of the annuity, any proceeds of the annuity are protected from the beneficiary's creditors. The annuity owner may thus protect the annuity from his creditors and also any creditors of his beneficiary. This can be particularly useful if the beneficiary is subject to the same potential claims as the annuity owner.

The only way that creditors can seize an annuity is if they can prove that the designation of beneficiaries was an attempt to defraud the creditors, as noted in the Swiss debt collection bankruptcy act. Fraud, however, is very difficult to prove. One scenario would be if the annuity and designation of the beneficiaries was made within six months of the date the annuity owner filed for bankruptcy. Another would be if it could be proven that the designation of beneficiaries was made with the intent to shield assets because the investor knew that he or she was about to declare bankruptcy. In this case, if the designation of beneficiaries was made within five years before the owner of the annuity declared bankruptcy or has his assets seized, creditors may be able to seize the annuity. Intent to defraud, though, would have to be proved.

Attempting to prove that an investor did in fact plan to defraud creditors could be established only under strict and specific circumstances. Most importantly, it would have to be shown that the annuity owner was in financial desperation -- meaning that he was already carrying an overload of debt -- and that he made the designation of beneficiaries in response to that indebtedness. On the other hand, fraud could not be proven if, at the time he or she bought the annuity and designated a beneficiary, the annuity owner had enough assets to cover his or her debts. Moreover, showing that he or she could not foresee the coming indebtedness would make it almost impossible for a creditor to prove fraud.

Swiss annuities are strongly protected from creditors. This includes the American IRS. If annuities are structured properly, and no intent to defraud can be proven, the annuities are virtually untouchable. Investors may be assured that their assets in the annuity are protected and that the proceeds of the annuity will remain intact.

Much of this protection arises from the fact that Swiss annuities are protected by Swiss law. For example, for a creditor to move ahead with a collection procedure against a foreign debtor's Swiss annuities, the creditor may seek to seize the assets of the debtor's annuity in Switzerland. If the creditor attempts to seize assets of the debtor in the debtor's home country, the creditor may file for the recognition of the foreign bankruptcy decree in Switzerland.

Nevertheless, no matter how the creditor may attempt to seize the assets of the annuity owner, the creditor's actions will be subject to Swiss law. The rules that oversee the protection of insurance policies will be in full effect. Since the investor owns a Swiss annuity, Swiss law now takes precedence over the laws that may govern collection efforts in his or her home country. It does not matter where the investor's home country is, or where he or she currently lives. If the investor owns a Swiss annuity, the rights included with the contract are considered to be in Switzerland. In effect, the investor's Swiss assets enjoy an excellent degree of protection.

Using Offshore Trusts, Annuities, and Portfolio Bonds

The only way creditors may seize a Swiss annuity is to prove that the investor bought the annuity and designated beneficiaries with the intent to defraud his or her creditors. And that is a difficult case to prove.

Even if creditors institute proceedings in the home country of the investor, for example the United States, and a judgment is passed, the judgment will not be recognized by Swiss law. No payments would be made by the Swiss insurance company to the creditor.

A Brief Summary of the Benefits of Swiss Annuities

Swiss annuities offer numerous benefits to investors. Although annuities can be purchased in many countries around the world, none can match the overall advantages Swiss annuities provide. Here are the major benefits:

- *Asset protection.* By irrevocably designating a third party as the beneficiary, or by revocably or irrevocably designating a spouse and/or descendants as beneficiaries, the policy owner is able to protect the policy from creditors. Provided that the annuity provides for payments to the beneficiary, and that beneficiary has not made any contribution to the purchase of the annuity, the annuity is also protected from potential creditors of the beneficiary. It should be noted that the asset protection is guaranteed by Swiss law and does not cost the investor anything. It comes with Swiss annuities. Virtually the only way a creditor can seize an annuity is to prove that the investor purchased the annuity with the intent to defraud the creditor. This is most difficult to prove in Swiss courts. Even if a judgment is rendered in another country, that judgment has no standing in Swiss courts. The Swiss

have a strong reputation for protecting the assets of their investors.
- *Financial safety.* Any investment sold in Switzerland is backed by the country's financial strength. Switzerland is considered by many authorities to be the financially strongest country in the world. Unlike the currencies of many other countries, including the United States, the Swiss franc is backed by gold. The Swiss insurance industry has not suffered a failure in over a century.
- *Swiss annuities offer excellent rates and dividends.* Because of Switzerland's advantageous tax rates and generally sound financial practices, Swiss annuities offer rates and dividends that are extremely competitive with annuities offered elsewhere.
- *Tax savings.* Swiss annuities, tied to the Swiss franc, are free from Swiss taxes.
- *Savings on fees.* Whereas many investments, trusts for example, have high fees and administration costs, Swiss annuities have no front-end or back-end load fees. Further, unlike annuities in other countries, the investor in Swiss annuities may cancel at any time with no loss of principal. Only if the annuity is canceled during the first year is a small penalty fee due. However, after the first year, all principal and interest and dividends are returned to the investor with no penalty. For many annuities around the world, cancellation times may extend up to five years.
- *Swiss privacy regarding finances.* Swiss annuities enjoy the famous Swiss privacy tradition. An annuity in Swiss francs is not subject to reporting to the U.S. Internal Revenue Service. In addition, the transfer of funds by wire or check are not reportable. Investors can be assured of the privacy of their accounts.
- *Ease of investing.* The Swiss have made management of a Swiss annuity simple. Investors can send deposits to Switzerland in U.S. dollars via a personal check. Funds

may also be transferred by bank wire. It is as easy as managing an annuity purchased and maintained in the United States.
- *Swiss annuities and U.S. pension plans.* Swiss annuities can be included in a variety of tax-sheltered plans in the United States. Some of these plans include IRAs, corporate plans, or Keogh plans. Investors have much flexibility.

Protecting Your Assets Through Swiss Annuities

Swiss annuities clearly provide many advantages and benefits to investors over annuities offered in other places. Still, perhaps most important, and often overlooked, is the superior asset-protection aspect of Swiss annuities. This aspect is a crucial point for investors who wish to ensure that their investments and growing wealth are protected from the claims of creditors.

When annuities are structured properly, Swiss law prevents, except in cases where intent to defraud can be proven, that annuities, along with other insurance policies, cannot be seized by creditors. These policies may not even be included in a Swiss bankruptcy proceeding.

Using A Swiss Insurance Broker

The only practical way for North Americans to get information on Swiss annuities is to send a letter to a Swiss insurance broker specializing in foreign business. This is because very few transactions can be concluded directly by foreigners either with a Swiss insurance company or with regular Swiss insurance agents. They can legally handle the business, but they aren't used to it.

Offshore Trusts

JML Swiss Investment Counsellors is an independent group of financial advisors. Since 1974 they have specialized in Swiss franc insurance, gold and selected Swiss bank managed investments for overseas and European clients. To date the group is servicing nearly 18,000 clients worldwide with investments through JML of more than 1 billion Swiss francs. Their services are free of charge to you because they are paid by the renowned companies with which you invest your money. Their commissions and fees are standard, and all transactions are subject to strict regulation by the Swiss authorities.

All of their staff are fluent in English, and understand the special concerns of the international investor. They know about all the many little details that are critical to you as a non-Swiss investor, and have answers to your tax questions and other legalities.

JML Jurg M. Lattmann AG
Swiss Investment Counsellors
Germaniastrasse 55, Dept. 212
CH-8033 Zurich, Switzerland
telephone: +41 1 368 8233
fax: +41 1 368 8299; marking the fax "Attn: Dept. 212"

or you may complete their online inquiry form at:

http://www.cyberhaven.com/JML/

When you contact a Swiss insurance broker, be sure to include, in addition to your name, address, and telephone number, your date of birth, marital status, citizenship, number of children and their ages, name of spouse, and a clear definition of your financial objectives including what dollar amount you would like to invest.

The Hybrid Company As An Alternative To The Trust

Company law concepts in the Isle of Man derive from English company law, and can have interesting results. Since England never had a concept of a separate non-profit company (or corporation), societies were formed as ordinary companies, under the same laws as commercial enterprises. Their character was differentiated by having members who guaranteed the debts of the company. Each member's guarantee might only be a penny, a shilling, or a pound, just as shares in a U.S. corporation might only have a nominal value of a tenth of a cent.

Generally, a "guarantee" company and a company with shares were very separate entities, but there was nothing in the company laws that actually prevented the two concepts from being combined in the creation of a single company. Thus the hybrid company was born.

This is not just an exotic exercise in ancient company law — it has some highly relevant uses for the wealthy investor. Where a trust would be impossible, or too restrictive, a hybrid company may function as a quasi-trust, for example:

- for a person living in a civil law jurisdiction that does not recognize trusts
- where the trust law is too restrictive for the desired purpose of the entity
- for family foundations or charities
- for persons living in countries where forced heirship laws determine who must inherit upon the owner's death.

The hybrid structure can be used to separate the legal ownership of the assets from the beneficial interest in them. Since the concept of a company is universal, even in those countries which do not recognize trusts, the hybrid company can solve problems where either the owner or the property is in such a country.

The documentation for the company should be drafted by an expert to accomplish the individual results desired. A typical example would be a situation in which the shareholding members fund the company's share capital and provide the company with its assets. The company's Articles of Association (equivalent to Articles of Incorporation or charter in other countries) provide that the company's management and control rest entirely in the hands of the shareholding members, via the election of the directors. But the shareholding members are excluded from receiving any benefit. The guarantee members have severely restricted rights and cannot vote for the directors, but they alone are eligible to benefit from dividend payments and interest-free or interest-bearing loans. Many variations of these rights are possible, depending upon individual needs.

The hybrid company is particularly useful for asset protection, since the shareholding member of the company can retain control over the assets but is legally excluded from receiving any benefit from them (making him the equivalent of the settlor of a trust, and is therefore provided with a means of protecting assets from potential future creditors. The guarantee members are the approximate equivalent of the beneficiaries of a trust.

Just one of the infinite variations of structure than can be created is the possibility of making guarantee memberships non-transferable and with no value in the hands of the heirs or creditors of the guarantee member.

Because the guarantee members are legally guarantors, not shareholders, they are not required to disclose either a shareholding or a beneficial interest in a trust.

Using Offshore Trusts, Annuities, and Portfolio Bonds

As I said at the beginning of this section, it is essential to use a qualified expert in this highly specialized area. My only recommendation is:

Skye Fiduciary Services Limited
Attn: New Clients Information
2 Water Street
Ramsey, Isle of Man 1M8 1JP
Great Britain
Telephone: +44 1624 816117
Fax: +44 1624 816645; attn: New Clients Information

(As most of my readers will know, the Isle of Man is a very useful tax haven separate from Great Britain, but since most of the world's post office won't know where it is, it is easier to humor them by including Great Britain in the address.)

Skye Fiduciary Services Limited are specialist consultants, designers of offshore and international fiduciary structures.

The chairman of the firm is Charles Cain, who was managing director of the second merchant bank to open on the Isle of Man, before he started his own business. He and his associates operate what I have no hesitation in calling the oldest and most experienced offshore corporate and trust management business in the Isle of Man.

In addition to hybrid companies, they can provide a full range of company management and trust management services. But it is their services in designing company and trust services that make them unique, and they can combine entities from several jurisdictions to create the most viable structure for the client. These can include trading companies, offshore family and charitable foundations, asset protection arrangements, and secure yet anonymous holding vehicles.

They also have the necessary expertise to ensure that offshore structures for U.S. persons precisely fit the required characterization under the Internal Revenue Code (and can develop tax efficient structures for those intending to immigrate to the U.S.).

Sources of Help for Offshore Investing

There seems to be a tendency in some circles to set up an offshore trust and then manage the assets themselves. This is not possible. It creates a sham, rather than a real trust. The solution is to use an asset management firm, which is an advantage for other reasons anyway. As professionals, they are in the markets constantly, and will generally do a much better job of managing investments. Not only does it create the arms length management required, but it frees one's time for enjoying life instead of looking after one's money. And with the trust structure, everything from illness to death can be handled by the trustees. There is always somebody to look after affairs in an emergency, and they are already in place and making management and investment decisions.

With that in mind, here are some of my personal recommendations of some of the world's best offshore service and investment management firms.

JML Swiss Investment Counsellors

One of the leaders in Swiss financial management is JML Swiss Investment Counsellors, a firm which offers a unique style of financial management. Clients can customize and control their own portfolios and still receive comprehensive management advice from some of the world's best experts on financial matters.

Recognizing that investors have differing goals, time frames, and tolerance for risk, JML's managers work with their individual clients to help them target their unique objectives. This naturally requires continued surveillance and analysis of worldwide economic trends, political events, financial markets, currencies, and other factors which could make some investments particularly attractive and others most unfavorable. Few individuals have the time or expertise to undertake this kind of evaluation themselves.

Further information about JML can be obtained by writing the following:

> JML Jurg M. Lattmann AG
> Swiss Investment Counsellors
> Germaniastrasse 55, Dept. 212
> CH-8033 Zurich, Switzerland
> telephone: +41 1 368 8233
> fax: +41 1 368 8299; marking the fax "Attn: Dept. 212"

or you may complete their online inquiry form at:

> http://www.cyberhaven.com/JML/

Weber Hartmann Vrijhof & Partners

Swiss investment managers are experienced in working with investors from around the world. Most are fluent in English and have substantial experience in managing various types of investments. They are comfortable managing an investor's entire portfolio if he wishes; however, for investors who prefer to make their own financial decisions, Swiss advisers are happy to offer their expertise to the degree it is required. They can help you manage your investments, or manage them for you - whichever arrangement makes you feel more comfortable. For the entrepreneur who devotes much of his energy to building his venture, the efficiency and competence of Swiss investment managers can be a major attraction.

Offshore Trusts

A fine example of a Swiss money management company is Weber Hartmann Vrijhof & Partners. Offering management services for the portfolios of both individuals and companies, the firm excels at providing personal attention to its clients. Weber Hartmann Vrijhof & Partners was established in 1992 and offers specialized investment services designed to meet the individual needs of their clients.

The minimum opening portfolio to be managed by this firm is $200,000 or equivalent. It is not feasible to manage an account of less than this as the transaction costs and inability to properly diversify would not allow a proper service to the client. The management team here normally recommends that a portion of the portfolio be invested in hard currencies other than the U.S. dollar including the Swiss franc, French franc, German mark, and Dutch guilder. Respected for their conservative approach to portfolio management, the partners assist clients with opening a custodial account at one of the major private Swiss banks, so that all client securities are held by the bank, not the investment manager.

A large percentage of their clients are based in the United States. One of their main goals has always been to get a certain portion of their clients' wealth out of the U.S. dollar and into European hard currencies such as Swiss francs, Deutschmarks, and Dutch guilders, and then build a portfolio with a mix of bonds and shares.

The Zurich-based executives you would be dealing with are Robert Vrijhof and René Schatt.

Robert Vrijhof began his banking career in 1978 with the Union Bank of Switzerland, working his way through the international securities trading department. Later, with Credit Suisse, he held the senior position as manager of the Foreign Stock Exchange trading section. In 1987, he accepted an offer by Foreign Commerce Bank as portfolio manager. His profound knowledge in this area soon led to the position of Vice-President and head of the portfolio management group at Focobank.

Using Offshore Trusts, Annuities, and Portfolio Bonds

René Schatt started his banking career in 1977 with the Thurgauer Cantonalbank, where he finished his basic training. In 1984, he joined the Foreign Commerce Bank and worked his way through the securities administration and trading department. At the same time, he continued studying and in 1987, he achieved the "Federal Diploma of Banking Expert." In 1990, he was promoted to Vice-President and head of the securities department. In 1992, he joined the first Korean Bank in Switzerland, KDB Bank (Switzerland) Ltd., working as Senior Vice-President and being the Swiss Member of the General Management.

If you wish to learn more about the services the firm offers, contact them at:

Weber Hartmann Vrijhof & Partners, Ltd.
Attn: New Clients Department
Zurichstrasse 110B
CH-8134 Adilswil
Switzerland
Tel: +41 1 709-11-15
Fax: +41 1 709-11-13, please mark fax "Attn: New Clients Department"

or you may use their online inquiry form at:

http://www.cyberhaven.com/whvp/

Even though many investors recognize that Switzerland is a center of finance and investment, they do not realize the vast scope of the investment options offered by Swiss financial institutions and companies. Switzerland is a prime spot for investment for numerous reasons, most importantly for the strength of its currency, security of its financial system, and steady returns on investment.

Offshore Trusts

Tax-Free Investing in the United States

Few Americans realize this, but the United States is considered a tax haven by many foreign investors. While U.S. citizens are struggling with federal, state, and local tax burdens of 40% or more of their total income, foreign investors often can invest in the United States tax-free or almost tax-free, and a properly structured trust is often a foreign investor for tax purposes. (The rules are complex, and proper professional advice must be sought before making any investments in the U.S.)

The country is not a straightforward no-tax haven like the Cayman Islands or the Bahamas. Instead, it has some complicated tax laws and tax treaties that, when taken together and fully understood, provide opportunities for the foreign investor to make low-tax gains in U.S. investments.

The United States encourages tax-free foreign investment because it needs foreign capital to finance the economy and the government budget deficit. For example, Congress generally imposes a 30% withholding tax on all interest payments to foreign residents and corporations. Foreign investors let it be known quickly that they would take their money elsewhere if the withholding tax remained, however, and exceptions to the tax now exist.

The great benefit of the U.S. tax haven for many foreigners occurs when the U.S. tax rules are combined with those of other countries. The United States taxes its citizens and residents on their worldwide income. But noncitizens and nonresidents are not taxed on income from certain sources within this country. As a result, there are a number of foreign individuals who invest in the U.S. in order to take advantage of these non-taxable situations.

Using Offshore Trusts, Annuities, and Portfolio Bonds

As a nonresident alien, you can get these benefits in many situations:

- No U.S. taxes on bank-deposit interest
- No U.S. tax on capital gains earned on U.S. stocks and bonds.

There will, however, be some tax on dividends from U.S. stocks.

In cases in which a tax might be incurred, such as on dividends, this often can be reduced or avoided by locating an offshore corporation in a country that has a favorable tax treaty with the United States. The Treasury Department has renegotiated a number of the tax treaties, but there still are some under which the U.S. withholding tax rate on dividends is significantly reduced.

Investing in U.S. real estate used to be an easy way to tax-free income and gains for nonresident aliens. But the rules were changed in 1980, and the profits no longer will be tax-free.

American Options Investing

Since capital gains are generally not taxable to foreigners, obviously any investing program which makes its profits in the form of capital gains, rather than dividends, interest or other types of earnings, is highly desirable. Unfortunately, there are not many such investing programs.

But one that does exist is trading options on stocks or on a stock index (such as the Standard & Poor's 500 Index). Since the gain or loss from trading in options is a capital gain, any profits made by a foreigner from trading in such options are free from any tax imposed by the United States.

As many investors already know, options are notoriously speculative and most people who try trading in them wind up losing money. Therefore, in order to take advantage of this tax benefit, it is first imperative to find a method of trading options which has a good probability of actually making money.

Almost any method of trading options which has the chance of making an above average return also carries a commensurate high degree of risk. But some practitioners of the arcane art of options trading do manage to do better than others over the years. One such person who has done very well for his clients is Max G. Ansbacher, Chairman of Ansbacher Investment Management, Inc.

Mr. Ansbacher has a long and distinguished involvement with options. In fact, he is the author of the first book published on the modern form of options, titled *The New Options Market, Revised and Enlarged Edition*. It was originally written in 1975 and Mr. Ansbacher has been trading options professionally ever since. In addition to this book, which has become one of the all time best selling books on options, he has written two other books on investing, has lectured on options at over 50 investment conferences in both the U.S. and overseas, and is the creator of The Ansbacher Index which is broadcast over the world wide facilities of the CNBC cable network.

He manages accounts for investors in both the U.S. and overseas. What sets Mr. Ansbacher apart from many others is that he has an excellent record of bringing in above average profits for his clients. Since most people who buy options seem to lose money, we asked Mr. Ansbacher what the key was to his success. He replied, "Yes, I agree that most people who buy options do seem to lose money. But what many people don't realize is that the money which the options buyers lose, doesn't disappear from the face of the earth. Rather it becomes the profits of the options *sellers*. And therefore, I concentrate in *selling* options."

What Mr. Ansbacher was saying is that options trading is actually a zero sum game when one looks at the total overall economic effect. This means that buying and selling options in its total impact on the economy does not either create any money or lose any money (except transaction costs). If the sellers make money, the buyers lose money. And if the buyers make money, then the sellers must lose money.

Since the options *buyers* tend to be the ones who lose money, it therefore must be true that the options *sellers* are the ones who make money over the long run. We asked Mr. Ansbacher why this should be true. His answer was, "The options buyers tend to be less sophisticated than the sellers. They don't always carefully assess the chances that their stocks will really go up enough to make money when they buy a call. Similarly, if people think a stock or a stock market is going to go down, they often over estimate how much it is going to go down. They will buy a put which is going to lose money unless the stock makes a really unusually large move within a relatively short period of time. These are the options I sell."

Of course there is not an investment program yet invented which makes money on every single trade, and option selling is no exception. When we asked Mr. Ansbacher about this, he said, "Certainly there are times when we have losses, but we believe that the probability lies with the sellers. And so we usually find that every loss is matched by many more winners."

Selling options is something which has to be done very carefully, because the risk is high. We asked Mr. Ansbacher what he does to control this risk. He said that the first defense was to control the number of options which he sells. "I usually sell only about one fifth the number of options which margin rules permit me to do. The second line of defense is that I use stop loss orders, which in most instances will automatically get me out of the options before the losses rise to a point which I consider unacceptable."

He continued, "The most interesting line of defense and the most important from the point of view of making money, is that I sell out-of-the-money options. This means that I sell options which have

Offshore Trusts

a strike price which is a distance away from the current price of the underlying security." We should point out that a strike price is the level at which an option becomes effective.

What Mr. Ansbacher means is that if a stock is 100, for example, he will not sell the 100 strike price call, because it is tool likely that the stock will go above 100 and he might lose money. Instead, he might sell the call with a strike price of 120. The stock would have to be above 120 at the option's expiration for the seller of the option to sustain a loss. Obviously it is less likely that a stock will go up 20 points than it will merely go up a few points. So, by selling out-of-the-money options, Mr. Ansbacher is able to shift the probabilities in his favor.

Another major decision which an options trader has to make is whether to be trading calls, which go up in price when a stock goes up, or puts which go up in price when the stock goes down. Mr. Ansbacher said that he makes this decision based upon a number of factors, including his long experience in the field. "One of the factors I rely upon, is my own Ansbacher Index. This Index tells me whether the puts or the calls are higher priced. Since I am selling these options, I will generally choose to sell the ones which are higher priced. I believe the Index also gives an indication of which way the stock market is likely to go in the intermediate future." Thus, Mr. Ansbacher can sell options on the stock market which will be profitable for his clients if the market moves as The Ansbacher Index indicates it is likely to do.

The minimum account which Mr. Ansbacher accepts is US$100,000, and he accepts accounts from people residing anywhere in the world. Depending upon the type of account, the investor will receive monthly or quarterly statements giving the exact value of the account. Clients are encouraged to discuss their accounts personally with Mr. Ansbacher.

For more information contact:

Ansbacher Investment Management, Inc.
Attn: New Clients Information
515 Madison Avenue, 29th Floor
New York NY 10022
telephone: (212) 308-2929
fax: (212) 308-0777; Attn: New Clients Information

Asset Allocation -- The Key To Successful Investing

One of the newest forms of investments in America is called asset allocation. Basically what it means is that one investment is "allocated" to a number of different types of investments by a professional investment allocator. The reason for this allocation is that no one type of investment is the best in all investment climates, and no one type of investment is usually appropriate for all of one person's investment money.

By using an asset allocation program, a person can invest a large amount of his principal in one place, gaining ease of tracking the investment, while attaining the advantage of having a number of different investments to serve his different investment objectives.

The asset allocator performs the service for the investor of allocating varying amounts of a total investment into different areas of investing, such as income stocks, growth stocks, small capitalization stocks, etc., and a variety of fixed income securities.

Offshore Trusts

For modest to medium-sized investments, one method of attaining even more diversification of investments, and expertise in the actual details of the investments, is to allocate the investment among various top-rated mutual funds. As is well known, mutual funds can perform a number of important tasks for the investor. Diversification among a large number of stocks is possible for even a relatively small sum of money. Expertise is available on any type of investment at a relatively low price. Last, there is great liquidity with ease of purchasing and selling.

The actual allocation into different mutual funds will depend upon three principal criteria:

1) What is the risk to reward profile of the individual investor,
2) What is the need of the investor for predictable current income as opposed to the desire for capital gains, and
3) What is the state of the economic and investment cycles at the particular moment in time.

The first and most important criteria are clearly the needs of the investor. These outweigh any thoughts of where any market may be going or where an allocator believes that the most money can be made. The first need which needs to be addressed is the risk which the investor is prepared to accept. All investment involves some degree of risk, but that risk can rage from the minor risk of how inflation can impact an investment in the next 90 days, to the risk of a high flying initial public offering in a company which may have no earnings and no prospect for earnings in the foreseeable future.

The amount of risk which is appropriate for an individual investor depends upon both the investors actual economic situation and his psychological attitudes towards risk of loss. Human temperament plays a very large role in determining risk tolerance. For example, if a person remembers a period of his or her past where they did not have enough money to make ends meet, they may be very adverse to taking any risk at all. Their attitude may be, "We worked hard for that money, and we don't want to lose it."

Others may have almost the opposite approach. They may never have known deprivation, and may have earned a good income all their life. Their attitude may be that they can live very well on their current earnings, and so any savings can be used to speculate. If the speculation turns out to be successful, that will be great and they can raise their standard of living even further. But if the speculation doesn't work out, that's OK too because they will simply continue living as they have.

Thus a good investment allocator will first determine what the needs of his clients are with respect to risk. One method is to determine first how much money is needed to maintain the current standard of living of the investor, and if he or she is not yet retired, how much of the investment will be needed when they do retire. Whatever amount is needed for these purposes is then designated as income producing principal and is invested accordingly into low-risk, high-yielding investments.

The balance can then be invested according to the investor's wishes into areas which can offer the promise of large capital gains in the future. This is the risk portion of the principal, and care must be taken so that the allocator and the investor agree on what amount of risk is to be taken.

The third and equally important task of allocating is to attempt to maximize the return to the investor from the changes in the economic cycle. When business has been in a slump and starts to turn up with both interest rates and inflation low, the largest profits are typically made in the stock market. But as the economy continues to expand, interest rates will rise and so will inflation. These factors make the prognosis for the economy less rosy, and the stock market may start to gyrate, and then fall. Perhaps gently at first and then more rapidly. So the stock market is definitely not the place to be.

Offshore Trusts

At the same time that the stock market is suffering from inflation, the price of hard assets such as gold, oil, and real estate could well be rising rapidly. It is in these areas that fortunes are made during inflationary periods in the economy.

And then as the economy finally begins to cool down due to the effect of high interest rates, interest rates will begin to fall nd the big money may be made by investing in long-term non-callable bonds.

Thus a good allocator must keep in mind the needs of the individual investor and the current status of the economy. And of course he must have an intimate familiarity with specific investments which are available to investors. Whether they be stocks, bonds, or fixed income securities, the allocator must know which are appropriate for the investor and which will likely do well in the present stage of the economy.

Our favorite allocator is Max G. Ansbacher, a man who has been a practicing lawyer and is still licensed to practice law. He has had over twenty years' experience with stocks and stock markets. He is the man we recommend for options in the section above, and his credentials in the stock market are equally impressive. The second book he wrote is titled *How to Profit from the Coming Bull Market* and it was published in the summer of 1981 near the bottom of the long bear market which had actually begun in 1973.

This book explained how and why a strong bull market was about to start on Wall Street. At the time it was published the book was largely ignored by a public which had grown cynical about a stock market which seemed to do nothing but go sideways or down, year after year.

But just one year after Mr. Ansbacher's book was published, the market suddenly took off like a rocket in August 1982 to start one of its greatest bull markets ever, and to establish Mr. Ansbacher's reputation as an insightful student of the stock market. Today Mr. Ansbacher heads up his own firm, Ansbacher Investment Management, Inc.

We recently asked Mr. Ansbacher what his philosophy was concerning asset allocation. He replied, "Asset allocation is probably the most important single aspect of any investment program. And yet what is so strange about it is that it is often not even considered by investors. Some people will have most of their money in the stock market most of the time, unaware of the large risks which the market sometimes contains. Others believe in bonds, and continue to invest most or all of their money there, apparently unaware that in the 1970's and early 1980's the bond market was the biggest money loser of any investment. I would say that asset allocation is not just important, it is the key to successful investing."

In view of the importance which asset allocation has, we wondered just how Mr. Ansbacher went about handling an asset allocation account for a client. "The first thing I do is to talk to the client in whatever depth is necessary to determine the proper risk profile for the client. This depends upon his current financial situation and what he foresees for his future situation as well as his psychological feelings towards money and the potential loss of money. The second thing I do is to make an outline of the client's need for current income. This naturally has a great deal of influence on how we can invest the funds."

"Only after this has been done, do I then discuss with the client where I think the financial markets are heading and where the best returns are likely to be made in the future. The first step in actually making the investments are to decide upon the proportion of money going into each class of investments. The second part is to select the actual investments. For a number of reasons, I select from among the thousands of mutual funds which are available in the U.S. They range all the way from bond to preferred stocks, to common stocks of all types. There is usually a time and a place for almost all of them, but we try to pick the best one for that particular client at that particular time in the client's life, and in the life of the markets."

Mr. Ansbacher explained that his minimum investment is $100,000, and that he works with some of the biggest mutual fund organizations in the U.S., including Fidelity, Dreyfus and other mutual fund management firms. He does not bill his clients for a fee or commission for the work he does, because his compensation is paid to him by the mutual funds.

We have always believed that to be a good asset allocator is one of the most difficult tasks in the investment world, because it requires so many different considerations. To see just what kind of factors Mr. Ansbacher considers we asked him how he would go about planning an asset allocation program for a client whom we made up.

We gave him as an example of a potential client, a 50-year-old German married man who earns the equivalent of $200,000 a year and has a well-funded pension plan with his company. He is in good health and plans to retire at about the age of 65. We asked Mr. Ansbacher to assume that this man comes to him with $300,000 to invest. Here is how Mr. Ansbacher went about making his asset allocation process.

Mr. Ansbacher thought out loud, "The first question I have is about the amount of $300,000. Since he has a pension plan with his company, it is obviously not pension money. It is also a rather large amount for a person earning $200,000 to want to invest in the U.S. Is it inherited money? Does his wife earn money? Is this his life savings? Did he make a successful investment? The reason I ask this question is that it is very important to know if the money is replaceable. If it is inherited, will there be more to follow, or is this all? First I would want to know whether there will be more money coming in or not."

"Second, I would want to know more about his potential future obligations. Do he or his wife having living parents or other relatives who may need financial support in the future? How much support, if any, does he expect that his children will need in the future? Does he have disability insurance or a company plan in case he becomes disabled before he retires? Is there some specific financial goal that he has, such as acquiring a vacation home, yacht or other item which will require a substantial amount of ready cash. All these factors related to the amount of risk which I would want to take."

"The next set of considerations center around his financial situation now. Since he lives in Germany, this means that he pays a high tax on income such as dividends and interest, but pays no capital gains tax. Right away that sways me into investments which are likely to have high capital gains. I would want to know whether the $200,000 he earns covers all of his current expenses, or whether his current standard of living is so high that he needs extra income each year."

"Once we have the answers to these questions, we can begin to solve the problem of how best to allocate this investment. If there are no likely financial needs coming up in the future, and if at the time of the investment I decide that the stock market is not over priced or likely to decline for other reasons, I would place most of the money into various stock funds. I am particularly fond of funds which use value investing, which means that they pick stocks based upon how large an amount of earnings one gets for each dollar invested. This is another way of saying that they seek out stocks with high quality and low price/earnings ratios."

"The reason I like value investing is that many studies have shown that low price/earnings stocks outperform other stocks in normal markets. And in down markets heir inherent value keeps them from falling as far as others. The second group of stocks I would pick would be senior growth stocks. This means stocks which grow year after year because they are gaining market share, or because they are in a solid growth industry. Examples of this are some pharmaceutical companies which are constantly creating new and better drugs, or highly efficient national retail chains which are constantly gaining market share over local competitors."

"One advantage which growth stocks have for this particular client is that they usually don't pay a very large dividend, which fits right in which his local tax structure. Depending upon the wishes of the client, we would consider some gold stocks as a hedge against

Offshore Trusts

inflation. And we might add some mutual funds which specialize in large capitalization companies, because these are the tried and proven winners among all the competition in the economy, and often outperform other stocks when the economy softens."

"I would also place a portion of the assets into a short or medium term bond fund for three reasons:

1) This could be a source of money in case an emergency arose which required a withdrawal from the fund,
2) It is a reserve in case some outstanding bargains come up for investment, and
3) It is a hedge against a downturn in the stock market."

Of course the actual percentage allocations would be discussed with the client. The actual funds selected would depend upon their performance records at the time of the investment. And in general, much of the allocation would depend upon the state of the economy at the time of the investment."

We thanked Mr. Ansbacher for sharing his thoughts with us, and for giving us an inside look at how he goes about this critically important task. We believe that he is one of the very best people working with investors to achieve their personal financial goals, through custom tailoring an investment allocation to their personal needs. Investors interested in using his services can contact him as follows:

Ansbacher Investment Management, Inc.
Attn: New Clients Information
515 Madison Avenue, 29th Floor
New York NY 10022
telephone: (212) 308-2929
fax: (212) 308-0777; Attn: New Clients Information

Last Words

We hope you close the pages of this book with a better understanding of the trust and how it can be put to practical use for you and your family.

The various trust forms described here can be forceful instruments when employed in the right way and under the proper circumstances. Your individual situation may even suggest the use of two or more trusts to best serve your special needs.

If you have learned anything here it should be that making plans for your economic future and for events after your death is a complex and technically demanding operation requiring the best talent available. You need experts. You do not need lawyers, accountants or insurance salesmen who practice estate planning on a part time basis, or who just happen to be your friends and acquaintances.

In planning your estate you should explore all the options, understand fully the possible ramifications of each recommended decision, and decide only when you are satisfied you know and understand where you are going. Second opinions are certainly in order. And once you establish your plan, be sure to continually review your financial health, just as you have regular medical check ups. Times and events change things, and your plan should always reflect those changes.

You work all your life to acquire property as a means to care for your family. Surely, a few hours spent in careful planning concerning your wealth is well worth the time.

In spite of government, taxes and life's adversities, is still possible to avoid the Bible's suggestion that man ". . . heapeth up riches and knoweth not who shall gather them.".

Glossary

acceptance - unconditional agreement to the terms of an offer resulting in a valid contract.

advance directive - a pre-written document addressed to health care providers expressing the signer's wishes concerning the type and extent of medical treatment to be rendered to that patient when in a terminal or extreme state of medical decline; also called a "living will." Compare "power of attorney."

agency - a relationship between a person (the "principal") who gives another (the "agent") the right to act in his or her behalf so as legally to bind the principal.

alimony - a spousal support allowance paid to one spouse by the other, pending or after a legal separation or divorce.

appreciation - the dollar amount by which the value of an asset increases.

articles of incorporation - a document filed with an appropriate government agency in order to incorporate a business.

attachment - the post-judicial civil procedure by which personal property is taken from its owner pursuant to a judgement or other court order.

bailment - the delivery of property by its owner (the "bailor") to another person (the "bailee") for some specific purpose, after the accomplishment of which, the property is returned to the owner.

basis - the original cost of an asset used to measure increased value for tax purposes.

beneficiary - one designated to receive income from a trust estate; a person named in an insurance policy to receive proceeds or benefits.

bequest - a gift of personal property by will, also called a "legacy."

capital gain - the amount of profit earned from the sale or exchange of property, measured against the original cost basis.

child custody - the right and duty to care for, control and provide maintenance of a child awarded to a person, usually a parent, as part of a divorce or separation proceeding.

child support - the obligation of a noncustodial parent to contribute economic support for a minor child, usually in periodic money payments.

civil law - the body of law based on Roman law and used in many non-English speaking nations, in the U.S. only in the state of Louisiana; as compared to the English "common law" system.

civil suit - a non-criminal legal action between parties relating to a dispute or injury seeking remedies for a violation of contractual or other personal rights.

codicil - a document supplementing or modifying an existing last will and testament.

common law - the large body of law developed in England from judicial decisions based on customs and precedent, constituting the basis of the present English, commonwealth and U.S. legal systems. See "equity."

community property - in certain states, property acquired during marriage jointly owned by both spouses, each with an undivided one half interest.

contract - a binding agreement between two or more parties; also the written or other evidence of such an agreement.

conversion - the crime of illegal and unauthorized use of another's personal property, usually involving money held in a fiduciary or other custodial capacity.

corporation - a business, professional or other entity recognized in law to act as a single legal "person," although composed of one or more natural persons, endowed by law with various rights and duties including the right of succession.

corpus - the property owned by a fund, trust or estate, also called the "principal."

creator - see "grantor."

creditor - one to whom a debtor owes money or other valuable consideration.

custodial account - a bank account opened on behalf of a minor, which becomes the property of the minor when he or she reaches the age of majority. The "custodian" is the fiduciary who manages the account, usually the one who creates it.

debtor - one who owes another (the "creditor") a money amount or other valuable consideration, especially one guilty of neglecting payment.

decedent - a term used in probate to describe a deceased person.

declaration - a formal statement in writing of any kind, often signed and notarized, especially a document establishing a trust; also in trust law called an indenture or agreement.

deed - a formal written document signed by the owner conveying title to real estate.

devise - a gift or disposition of real property in a last will and testament; the person receiving real property by will is a "devisee."

divorce - a judicial declaration ending a valid marriage, usually apportioning debts and property and deciding issues of child custody, support and spousal maintenance.

domicile - a person's permanent legal home, as compared to a place that may be only a temporary residence.

durable power of attorney - see "power of attorney."

employee - one who works for another, the "employer": for purposes of workers' compensation laws, any person earning wages, salary, or commissions, not including farm workers, domestic servants, people working for a spouse or parent, railroad employees and independent contractors.

equity - a body of judicial rules developed under the common law used to enlarge and protect rights and enforce duties while seeking to avoid unjust constraints and narrowness of statutory

law; also the unrealized value of a person's investment or ownership, as in a trust beneficiary's "equitable interest."

estate - any of various kinds or types of ownership a person may have in real or personal property; often used to describe property of a deceased person, meaning the assets and liabilities remaining after death.

estate tax - taxes imposed at death by the federal and most state governments on all assets of a decedent, except on the first $600,000 in value which is exempt.

executor - a person who manages the estate of a decedent, also called an "executrix" if a female, "personal representative," "administrator," or "administratrix."

exemption - in tax law, a statutory defined right to avoid taxes; also the statutory right granted to a debtor in bankruptcy to retain a portion of his or her real or personal property free from a creditor's claims.

family partnership - a legal business relationship created by agreement among two or more family members for a common purpose, often used as a means to transfer income and assets among family members so as to limit individual personal liability and taxes; see "partnership" and "limited partnership."

fiduciary - a person holding property in trust for another, as a trustee, guardian or executor of an estate.

future interest - an interest in property, usually real estate, possession and enjoyment of which is delayed until some future time or event.

gift tax - a U.S. federal tax imposed on any gift made by one person to another person annually in excess of $10,000.

grantor - a person who conveys real property by deed; also a person who creates a trust, also called a trust "donor," "settlor," or "trustor."

gross estate - the total value for estate tax purposes of all a decedent's assets.

guardianship - a power conferred on a person, the "guardian," usually by judicial decree, giving them the right and duty to provide personal supervision, care and control over another person who is unable to care for himself because of some physical or mental disability.

homestead exemption - a state statutory exemption of one's home place from certain taxes or from creditor claims in bankruptcy, particularly generous in Florida and Texas.

indices of ownership - factors indicating a person's power over, therefore ownership especially of trust property, including revocability.

income beneficiary - the life tenant in a trust.

incorporation - the registration and qualification process by which a corporation is formed under state law.

indemnity - an agreement by which one promises to protect another from any loss or damage, usually describing the role of the insurer in insurance law.

indenture - a basic document setting out the terms of a trust; also a formal contract by which one obligates himself to serve another for a period of time; see also "declaration."

infant - legal description of a person under 18 years of age.

inheritance tax - a tax imposed by many states on the amount a person receives from a decedent's estate, rather than on the estate itself.

insurance - a contract or "policy" under which a corporation, known as an "insurer," undertakes to indemnify or pay a person, the "insured," for a specified loss in return for the insured's payment of a "premium."

inter vivos trust - Latin for "between the living," meaning a "living trust."

intestate - the condition of a person who dies without making a last will and testament, in which case the person's property is distributed to next of kin according to the state law of the deceased's residence; see "testator."

irrevocable trust - a trust which, one established by the settlor, cannot be ended or terminated by the settlor.

joint tenancy - a form of property co-ownership in which parties hold equal title with the right of survivorship; a "joint tenancy by the entireties" is a similar tenancy reserved to husband and wife.

judgement - an official and authenticated decision of a court.

jurisdiction - the statutory authority a court exercises; also a word used to describe the geographic or subject matter area over which a court has power.

last will and testament - a written document in which a person directs the post mortem distribution of his or her property. State law governs the specific requirements for a valid will.

legacy - a gift of money or personal property by will, also called a "bequest," the recipient being the "legatee."

legal capacity - the competency or ability of parties to make a valid contract, including being of majority age (18 years) and of sound mind.

life insurance trust - an irrevocable living trust that holds title to a policy on the settlor's life, proceeds from which are not part of the settlor's estate.

life estate - the use and enjoyment of property granted by the owner to another during the owner's life, or during the life of another, at the termination of which, title passes to another

known as the "remainderman."

living trust - see "inter vivos trust."

living will - see "advance directive."

limited partnership - a partnership in which individuals known as "limited partners" have no management role, but receive periodic income and are personally liable for partnership debts only to the extent of their individual investment.

malpractice - tortuous, compensable professional misconduct or lack of professional skill resulting in injury to another, especially when applied to lawyers, health care providers, and other people trained in a profession.

marital deduction - the right under federal law of one spouse to pass on all property owner at death to the surviving spouse free of any tax.

marriage - the legal and religious institution whereby a man and women join in a binding contract for the purpose of founding and maintaining a family.

marriage, common law - the legal status recognized in some states when a man and a woman, although not legally wed, intend to marry, treat each other and present themselves to the public as though married, and live together for a minimum period of time, sharing property and earnings.

minor - see "infant."

minor's trust - an irrevocable trust established for the benefit of a minor, usually terminable at majority.

mortgage - the legal process (also the written document) by which a buyer or owner of real property (the "mortgagor") conditionally transfers title to a lender (the "mortgagee") as security for a loan to finance the purchase of, or improvements to the property, the condition being that the transfer becomes void upon full payment or performance according to the stipulated terms.

negotiable instrument - any written evidence of ownership of money or property, title to which is capable of being transferred from one person by delivery to another with or without endorsement, such as a promissory note or check; see "commercial paper."

offer - a written or verbal promise by one person (the "offeror") to another (the "offeree") to do or not to do some future act, usually in exchange for a mutual promise. See "acceptance" and "contract."

option - a contract provision allowing one to purchase property at a set price within a certain time period.

partnership - an association of two or more persons formed to conduct business for mutual profit. See "limited partnership."

policy - in insurance law, the contract between insurer and insured; see "insurance."

pour-over will - a will that directs assets not already given to an existing living trust shall go into that trust at the settlor's death.

power of attorney - a written instrument allowing one to act as agent for another, the scope of agency power indicated by the terms, known as "general" or "limited"; a "durable power of attorney," allowed in some states, appoints a person to act as an "attorney in fact" to make all medical decisions, including the withholding of life support when the person is unable to make decisions for himself because of illness or injury; see also "living will" and "advance directive."

premarital agreement - a contract between a man and woman prior to marriage, setting forth the division of their property in event of a divorce.

preservation trust - any trust designed to limit a beneficiary's access to income and principal.

primary residence - especially in tax law, a home place, as compared to a vacation or second home; see "domicile."

probate - a series of judicial proceedings, usually in a special court, initially determining the validity of a last will and testament, then supervising the administration or execution of the terms of the will and the decedent's estate.

property - any thing of value capable of being owned, including land (real property) and personal property, both tangible and intangible.

quit claim deed - a deed transferring any interest a grantor may have in real property without guarantees of title, if in fact any interest does exist.

real estate - land and any thing growing or erected thereon or permanently attached thereto.

real estate investment trust - also called an "REIT," an investment fund in trust form that owns and operates real estate for share holding investors who are the beneficiaries.

remainder - in testamentary law, the balance of an estate after payment of legacies; in property law, an interest in land or a trust estate distributed at the termination of a life estate. The person with a right to such an estate is the "remainderman."

rescind - cancellation or annulment of an otherwise binding contract by one of the parties.

retained interest trust - see "grantor trusts."

revocable trust - a living trust in which the settlor retains the power to revoke or terminate the trust, returning the corpus to himself.

right of survivorship - an attribute of a joint tenancy that automatically transfers ownership of the share of a deceased joint tenant to surviving joint tenants without the necessity of probate.

royalty trust - similar to an investment trust, but here a trust created by an oil or gas company, with shareholders benefitting from profits.

second to die insurance - a life insurance policy that does not pay proceeds until a second person, usually a surviving spouse dies.

separation - the cessation of a husband and wife living together by mutual agreement or by judicial decree, often as a prelude to a divorce; a separation agreement is a document governing the obligations and rights of a husband and wife who are separated.

settlor - see "grantor."

sole proprietorship - the conduct of an unincorporated business when an individual owns all business assets and is personally liable for all debts and obligations.

spendthrift trust - a restricted trust created to pay income to a beneficiary judged by the trust settlor to be too improvident to handle his or her own personal economic affairs.

sprinkle trust - a trust provision granting the trustee discretionary powers to distribute income and principal.

tenancy by the entireties - a joint tenancy between husband and wife, with the right of survivorship.

testator - a male who has made a last will and testament; a "testatrix" is a female who has done so.

trust - a legal device allowing title to and possession of property to be held, used, and/or managed by one person, the "trustee," for the benefit of others, the "beneficiaries."

ward - a minor child for whom a court has appointed a guardian; see also "infant" and "minor."

will - see "last will and testament."

will, holographic - a will written in the handwriting of the testator

About the Author

Over the past 25 years, Adam Starchild has been the author of over two dozen books, and hundreds of magazine articles, primarily on business and finance. His articles have appeared in a wide range of publications around the world — including Business Credit, Euromoney, Finance, The Financial Planner, International Living, Offshore Financial Review, Reason, Tax Planning International, The Bull & Bear, Trust & Estates, and many more.

Now semi-retired, he was the president of an international consulting group specializing in banking, finance and the development of new businesses, and director of a trust company.

Although this formidable testimony to expertise in his field, plus his current preoccupation with other books-in-progress, would not seem to leave time for a well-rounded existence, Starchild has won two Presidential Sports Awards and written several cookbooks, and is currently involved in a number of personal charitable projects.

His website is at http://www.adamstarchild.com

End Notes

1. Krensky v. De Swarte, 82 N.E. 2d 168, 171, 335 Ill. App. 435.
2. Sinclair v. Allender, 26 N.W. 2d 320, 325, 238 Iowa 212.
3. Pratt v Board of Ed. of Dist. No. 61, Kankakee County, 63 N.E. 2d 275, 281, 326 Ill. App. 610.
4. Wise v. Delaware Steeplechase & Racing Assn., 39 A. 2d 212, 217, 28 Del. Ch. 161.
5. Harvard College v Amory, 9 Pick. 446 (Mass., 1830).
6. *The American Fiduciary's Investment Problem* (Boston: Vance, Sanders & Co., 1951), p. 9.
7. Lovett v. Farnham, 169 Mass. 1, 6, 47 N.E. 246 (1897).
8. Humbird v. Humbird, 162 Md. 582, 160 Atl. 623 (1932).
9. Sheridan v. Riley, 133 N.J. Eq. 288, 32 A.2d 93 (1943).

Asset Protection Through Swiss Life Insurance Policies

by Marc Sola

This analysis is applicable to all life insurance policies that have been recognized by the supervisory authority, the Federal Office for Private Insurance Matters (Bundesamt für Privatversicherung), as well as to life insurance policies linked to mutual funds and derivatives. Annuities, fixed or variable, are treated as life insurance policies under Swiss law and are exempt from Swiss taxes. It should be noted at the outset that both legal entities and natural persons may be designated as beneficiaries under Swiss law. With respect to certain annuities and insurance companies, the policyholder may be a legal entity. The person insured, however, must in all cases be a natural person.

Using Offshore Trusts, Annuities, and Portfolio Bonds

OVERVIEW OF ASSET PROTECTION IN SWITZERLAND

Beneficiaries Are All-Important

When a person residing outside of Switzerland (hereinafter referred to as the „policy owner") purchases a life insurance policy from a Swiss insurance company and designates his or her spouse and/or descendants as beneficiaries of the policy, or irrevocably designates any other third party as beneficiary (e.g., a legal entity such as a trust), the insurance policy is protected by Swiss law against any debt collection procedures instituted by the creditors of the policy owner and also is not included in any Swiss bankruptcy procedure in this regard. Even when a foreign judgment or court order expressly decrees the seizure of the policy or its inclusion in the estate in bankruptcy, the policy may not be seized in Switzerland or included in the estate in bankruptcy.

Beware Fraudulent Conveyance

Creditors may only seize the policy or have it included in the estate in bankruptcy when the purchase of the policy or the designation of the beneficiaries is considered to be a fraudulent conveyance under Swiss law. This condition is fulfilled when the policy owner has designated the beneficiaries not more than one year before the initiation of debt collection proceedings that eventually lead to a bankruptcy decree against the policy owner or to the seizure of the policy owner's assets.

This condition is also met when the beneficiary has been designated with the clear intent to damage creditors or to treat some creditors more favorably than others and the designation was made within five years from the date debt collection proceedings resulting in a bankruptcy decree or in the seizure of assets were initiated against the policyholder. The creditors concerned, however, need to prove not only the policy owner's intent—and here we can see where the law stands—but also that the beneficiary had knowledge of the intent to defraud. Clearly such an intent to defraud cannot be proved when the beneficiaries were designated at a time the policy owner was solvent and no creditors had yet asserted any claims against him or her that could have rendered him or her insolvent.

When the policy owner has designated his or her spouse and/or descendants as beneficiaries, the insurance policy will be protected from claims made by his or her creditors irrespective of whether the designation is revocable or irrevocable. The policy owner may therefore designate his or her spouse and/or descendants as beneficiaries on a revocable basis and later revoke this designation prior to the expiration of the policy if at such time there are no threats from any creditors. At the expiration of the insurance policy the policyholder will be able to collect the proceeds pursuant to the policy, extend the existing policy, or roll the proceeds over into a new policy. It should be noted that if, at the time of expiration, a creditor appears or the owner becomes insolvent, a new policy would not be protected whereas an extended policy would.

Protection Even Under Duress

When an insurer receives a letter from the policy owner revoking the beneficiary designation (in connection with a foreign court order to revoke a past beneficiary designation in order to include the respective assets in a foreign bankruptcy estate), the insurer may come to the conclusion that the instruction received from the policy owner does not express the policy owner's true intent and was forced upon him or her by the foreign judge or court. The Swiss insurance company can only act upon orders of the owner if his or her actions are deemed not to have been made under duress. If there is any evidence that an order has been forced upon the owner, the insurance company cannot follow the instructions so issued. In such a case, the beneficiaries should inform the insurance company.

Automatic Protection in Case of Bankruptcy

In case of bankruptcy of the policy owner, protection is also guaranteed because ownership is transferred to the beneficiaries automatically. Any instructions from the original policy owner that are forced upon him or her can no longer be acted upon; only his or her beneficiaries, as the new owners, can give instructions to the insurance company.

ANALYSIS OF SWISS ASSET PROTECTION LAWS

Conditions for the Protection of Life Insurance Policies in Swiss Debt Collection and Bankruptcy Proceedings

According to the Swiss Insurance Act, a life insurance policy is protected from the policy owner's creditors under the following conditions.

Irrevocable Designation of Third Party as Beneficiary. According to Article 79 paragraph 2 of the Swiss Insurance Act, if the policy owner has irrevocably designated a third party as beneficiary of a life insurance policy, the policy may not be seized by the policy owner's creditors.[1] In the cited decision, the Federal Supreme Court held the following with regard to the effects of an irrevocable designation of a third-party beneficiary:

> In case of enforcement measures against the policy owner, if the designation of the beneficiary is irrevocable, there is in the estate of the policy owner no insurance claim and the policy owner has no right to revoke the beneficiary's right as normally would be the case. The creditors of the policy owner may, therefore, not seize, have listed or auction off [an insurance policy]. This principle is expressed in Art. 79 para. 2 Swiss Insurance Act according to which, if the policy owner has waived his or her right to revoke the designation, then the insurance policy may not be seized by the policy owner's creditors.[2] [Translation from the original French text]

According to Article 77 paragraph 2 of the Swiss Insurance Act, the designation of a third party as beneficiary will only be considered to be irrevocable if the policy owner has waived his or her right to revoke the designation in writing and the policy is physically handed over to the beneficiary.[3] By signing the relevant declaration and handing the insurance policy over to the beneficiary, the policy owner will meet these requirements.

Designation of Spouse and/or Descendants as Beneficiaries. If the policy owner has designated his or her spouse and/or descendants as beneficiaries of the insurance policy in question, according to Article 80 of the Swiss Insurance Act the policy may not be seized by his or her creditors[4] unless the policy owner has explicitly granted a security interest in the policy to a creditor.[5] The designation of the spouse and/or descendants as beneficiaries is not subject to specific formal requirements.[6] Regarding Articles 80 and 81 of the Swiss Insurance Act, the Federal Supreme Court held the following:

> Art. 80 and 81 of the Swiss Insurance Act provide for a special rule where the spouse and the descendants of the policy owner are beneficiaries of an insurance policy. The designation as beneficiary may no longer be revoked when the policy owner is declared bankrupt as would normally be the case in accordance with Art. 79 para. 1 of the Swiss Insurance Act. Pursuant to Art. 80 of the Swiss Insurance Act the claim against the insurer may not be subject to enforcement measures and the beneficiaries at the time when bankruptcy is declared will enter into the rights and obligations of the insurance agreement replacing the policy owner (pursuant to Art. 81 of the Act), unless they expressly decline such transfer of the agreement. Naturally, eventual liens of third parties relating to the insurance policy will not be concerned thereby (Art. 80 of the Swiss Insurance Act).[7]
> [Translation from the original German text]

In contrast to the designation of another third party as beneficiary; it is irrelevant in the case of the designation of a spouse and/or descendants whether the designation is irrevocable or revocable. The insurance policy will also be protected from the policy owner's creditors if the designation of the spouse and/or descendants is revocable.[8] If the policy owner falls into bankruptcy or if the debt collection office certifies to his or her creditors after a seizure that the assets seized do not cover the policy owner's debts, any spouse and/or descendants who are beneficiaries of the policy will, according to Article 81 of the Swiss Insurance Act, be assigned all the rights and duties of the policy owner under the relevant insurance policy.[9]

Rules on Fraudulent Conveyance

According to Article 82 of the Swiss Insurance Act, however, creditors of a policy owner may seize the policy even in the above cases if they can prove that the irrevocable designation of a third party or the designation of the spouse and/or descendants as beneficiaries is to be viewed as a fraudulent conveyance within the meaning of Article 285 *et seq.* of the Swiss Debt Collection and Bankruptcy Act.[10] The purchase of an insurance policy and the designation of beneficiaries are considered a voidable preference under the Swiss fraudulent conveyance rules in the following cases.

Designation Made Within One Year Before Bankruptcy or Seizure. According to Article 286 of the Swiss Debt Collection and Bankruptcy Act, gifts or gratuitous settlements made by a debtor are a voidable preference when the debtor is declared bankrupt or the debtor's assets are seized within one year after the initial transaction was made.[11] In calculating the one-year period, the duration of certain specific time periods will be added (the duration of preceding composition proceedings; the duration of a stay of opening a bankruptcy; in proceedings to liquidate an estate, the period between the date of decease and the liquidation order and the duration of preceding enforcement proceedings).[12] Because the gratuitous designation of a third party as beneficiary under an insurance policy can be regarded as a gratuitous transfer to that third party, such a designation may be voided by the creditors if it was effected within this one-year period.[13]

Designation Made with the Intent to Damage Creditors. According to Article 288 of the Swiss Debt Collection and Bankruptcy Act, all transactions are voidable that the debtor carried out during the five years prior to the seizure of assets or the opening of bankruptcy proceedings with the intention, apparent to the other party of putting his or her creditors at a disadvantage or of favoring certain of his or her creditors to the disadvantage of others.[14] The five-year period may be extended by the periods of Article 288a mentioned above. If the designation of the spouse and/or the descendants or of a third party was made with the specific intent of the debtor to damage creditors and the beneficiaries knew of this intent, the designation is also voidable.[15] To void the transfer, the creditors concerned need to prove the intent as well as the beneficiary's knowledge. It is, however, not sufficient for the proof of such intent to demonstrate that the designation took place at a time at which the policy owner was—due to his or her professional activities or investments—aware of certain risks as long as the policy owner's assets still covered all his or her debts and he or she could not foresee an insolvency.[16]

Protection of Foreigners Who Purchase Swiss Life Insurance Policies
The following rules regarding debt collection and bankruptcy procedures against foreigners in Switzerland apply only to assets located in Switzerland. It is important to note that the rights under an insurance contract between a foreigner and a Swiss insurance company are, according to Swiss law, deemed to be located at the domicile of the Swiss insurance company.[17] If the policy owner's and the beneficiaries' rights are embodied in a policy that must be considered as a security, however, a creditor could claim that the security could be seized in accordance with the debt collection and bankruptcy rules of the country in which the security is deposited, because securities normally are subject to the debt collection and bankruptcy law of the country in which they are deposited. This problem, however, can be avoided if the insurance policy is deposited in Switzerland.

Debt Collection and Bankruptcy Procedures Against Foreign Debtors. According to Article 275 of the Swiss Debt Collection and Bankruptcy Act, only assets that a creditor can seize in a debt collection procedure can be attached.[18] Because this principle also applies to foreign debtors,[19] a Swiss insurance policy purchased by a foreigner is protected

Asset Protection Through Swiss Life Insurance Policies

under the conditions set forth above.[20] Therefore, if creditors do not file for an attachment but rather for the recognition of a foreign bankruptcy decree, the insurance policy is nevertheless protected. According to Article 170 IPRG, the debtor's assets in Switzerland will be auctioned off for the benefit of his or her creditors in accordance with Swiss bankruptcy rules.[21] The rules in Article 79 Section 2 and Article 80 VVG described previously are part of these rules.[22]

Because debt collection and bankruptcy procedures in Switzerland are always based on Swiss bankruptcy rules alone, and these rules include Article 79 Section 2 and Article 80 VVG, life insurance policies are protected in accordance with Swiss law in such procedures, even when the debt collection or bankruptcy law in the debtor's domicile would not afford him or her such protection. In particular, according to Article 171 IPRG, only the Swiss rules on fraudulent conveyance apply, so the designation of beneficiaries cannot be avoided by creditors unless they prove that the conditions for fraudulent conveyance described previously are met, even if the purchase or designation was a voidable preference under the fraudulent conveyance rules applicable in the debtor's domicile.[23]

The creditors of a person residing outside of Switzerland, therefore, may not in Switzerland seize or include in the estate in bankruptcy any life insurance policies that are protected under Swiss law even if they have a judgment or a bankruptcy decree that is enforceable in Switzerland, unless they can prove that the designation of the beneficiaries of the insurance policy is a voidable preference under Swiss fraudulent conveyance rules.

Revocation of Beneficiary Designation by Order of Foreign Judge. A foreign judge or court may order a policy owner to revoke a past beneficiary designation in order to include the respective assets in the foreign bankruptcy estate. To comply with such an order or judgment, the policy owner may inform the insurer that he or she revokes the prior beneficiary designation. The question arises whether under Swiss law the insurer has to comply with such an instruction by the policy owner, which was forced upon him or her by a foreign judge or court.

In the event of an irrevocable designation of a third party under Article 79 Section 2 VVG, an insurer will not comply with the instruction by the policy owner because this would contradict the irrevocability of the beneficiary designation.

In the event of a revocable designation of the spouse or descendants, the spouse and descendants of a policy owner automatically succeed into the rights and obligations arising from the insurance contract at the moment when the policy owner is declared bankrupt, unless they expressly object to such succession.[24] The spouse or descendants have to inform the insurer accordingly.[25] Therefore, if the foreign policy owner has been declared bankrupt previously and later instructs the insurer that the beneficiary designation is revoked, the insurer will refuse to comply with such an instruction because at this time the rights and obligations arising from the insurance policy were already assigned to the beneficiary. In this context, it is important to make sure that the insurer in fact knows about the foreign bankruptcy decree and that the beneficiaries inform the insurer of their succession under Article 81 Section 2 VVG. Moreover, if an insurer receives a letter from the policy owner revoking the beneficiary designation, the insurer may come to the conclusion that the instruction received does not express the policy owner's true intent and was forced upon him or her by the foreign judge or court.

Under Article 18 of the Swiss Code of Obligations (CO), in case of a discrepancy between the real intent and the intent expressed in writing, a person who receives such a writing and knows that it does not express the real intent normally has to follow the real intent and ignore the writing. Although there is no court precedent dealing specifically with this situation, it is a general principle of Swiss law that a person who receives a written declaration of another person has to give the declaration the meaning that complies with the real intent of that person, if he or she knows the real intent. In other words, if an insurer receives a writing from a policy owner that he or she knows does not reflect the real intent, it can and has to ignore the writing.

TREATMENT OF FOREIGN ANNUITIES UNDER U.S. TAX LAW

No Excise Tax

Unlike many other foreign annuities, Swiss annuities are not subject to the 1 percent U.S. excise tax on the purchase of foreign annuity and insurance premiums. This is a by-product of the adoption in 1998 of a new Swiss-U.S. Double Tax Treaty and applies to premiums paid by a U.S. citizen to an insurance company domiciled in Switzerland.

Income on Foreign Fixed Annuities Can Be Taxable

Most foreign fixed annuities are no longer tax deferred in the United States (see Internal Revenue Service regulations, "Tax Treatment of Certain Annuity Contracts," Internal Revenue Code (Code) Sections 163(e) and 1271 through 1275). Under the rules of Code Section 1275, a Swiss fixed annuity is a debt instrument, that is, a „promise to pay a sum certain," in addition to being an insurance contract. Accordingly, the owner of a Swiss fixed annuity (as well as other foreign annuities that are seen as debt instruments) pays tax on the income that accrues, including currency gains if the annuity is denominated in a foreign currency.

Most tax experts agree that as a result of the loss of tax deferral, distributions prior to age 59 1/2, including loans against the policy, are not subject to the 10 percent penalty for early withdrawals. Thus it is possible to take tax-free withdrawals from a Swiss fixed annuity whenever the policyholder chooses.

Income on Foreign Variable Annuities Can Be Tax Deferred
Death Benefits in Policy Do Not Make It a Debt Instrument. The inside buildup of a foreign variable annuity continues to be tax free. The death benefits included in the policies do not make the annuities „debt instruments" (promises to pay a sum certain) and, therefore, are not tax deferred under Code Section 1275. They do not constitute debt instruments because they promise to pay a designated sum only if the

owner dies. There is no guarantee of a particular sum if the owner cashes in the policy while he or she is alive.

In addition to the above criteria for determining whether a variable annuity is a debt instrument, two further conditions need to be met for tax deferral.

1. *The Variable Annuity Must Not Be Self-Directed.* The income from a variable annuity is tax free if the owner (or his or her adviser) is not managing the investments himself or herself (a so-called "self-directed" annuity). Owners are permitted to choose investment categories, but under the self-directed annuity rules they may not choose the actual investments. If they do, they are treated as the owners of the underlying assets and the income generated by those assets is taxable.

2. *The Variable Annuity Must Be Adequately Diversified.* Finally, the inside buildup of variable annuities is tax free if the underlying portfolio is adequately diversified as defined in the U.S. tax code. An account meets the „diversification rule" if

    a. No more than 55 percent of the value of the total assets of the account is represented by any one fund;

    b. No more than 70 percent of the value of the total assets of the account is represented by any two funds;

    c. No more than 80 percent of the value of the total assets of the account is represented by any three funds; and

    d. No more than 90 percent of the value of the total assets of the account is represented by any four funds.

To make certain that variable annuities comply with the diversification rule at all times, portfolio rebalancing is required on at least a quarterly basis.

Asset Protection Through Swiss Life Insurance Policies

The tax-deferred status of Swiss variable annuities has consequences for early withdrawal just as do U.S. contracts. Swiss variable annuities, however, offer a combination of asset protection, a choice of asset allocation strategies based on an investor's risk profile and other needs, and tax deferral for U.S. investors. This makes them ideal long-term investments that can harness the power of compound growth for a retirement portfolio. See the following chart, Overview of Swiss Annuity Investments.

Overview of Swiss Annuity Investments			
Investment/ Feature	Fixed Annuity	Self-Directed Variable Annuity	Variable Annuity Portfolio
Annual Returns*	2.5% plus profit sharing dividends	Varies, with a wide range of first-class mutual funds to choose from	Fixed income 6% Conservative 7% Balanced 15% Dynamic 19%
Asset Protection	Yes	Yes	Yes
U.S. Tax Deferral	No	No	Yes

*For the variable annuity portfolio, returns are based on historic performance over five years, in part measured by index performance, that is, returns are indicative and cannot be guaranteed.

©Copyright 1999 JML AG, Zug

Editor's Comment: One of the concerns many practitioners have had concerning the use of Swiss annuities was that in cases of large annuities and/or annuities purchased by large estates, the designation of the spouse and/or children as beneficiaries of the annuity usually would not be consistent with a sound estate plan. Therefore, although the asset protection aspect of the annuity was attractive, the estate planning limitations were a hindrance. Now that it is clear that an „entity" can be named as irrevocable beneficiary of a Swiss annuity on the annuitant's death the estate planning concerns could be eliminated by naming the individual's estate planning trust as the beneficiary. Note, however, that if a nongrantor trust is named as the lifetime owner, the tax deferral (for variable annuities) will be lost because of the application of Code Section 72(u).

END NOTES

1. Decision of the Federal Supreme Court, BGE 112 II 157; MAURER, SCHWEIZERISCHES PRIVATVER-SICHERUNGSRECHT, 3d ed., Bern 1993, at 453; B. WIRET, PRIVATVERSICHERUNGSRECHT 3d ed., Zürich 1991, at 210, 212.
2. Federal Supreme Court, BGE 112 II 157.
3. BGE 85 III 58; Maurer, supra St 453; NÜNLIST, WEGLEITUNG ZUM NEUEN SCHULDBETREIBUNGS- UND KONKURSRECHT, 4th ed., Bern 1997, at 112.
4. Wiret, supra at 214; AMONN/GASSER, GRUNDRISS DES SCHULDBETREIBUNGS- UND KON-KURSRECHTES, 6th ed., Bern 1997, at 172 et seq.; JAEGER AND ROELLI, KOMMENTAR ZUM SCHWEIZERISCHEN BUNDESGESETZ ÜBER DEN VERSICHERUNGSVERTRAG, Bern 1993, at 214; BGE 59 III 203.
5. CARRON, LA LOI FEDERALE SUR LE CONTRACT DE L'ASSURANCE, Freiburg 1997, at 169.
6. Wiret, supra at 209.
7. Federal Supreme Court, BGE 105 III 133.
8. FRITZSCHE AND WALDER, SCHULDBETREIBUNG UND KONKURS NACH SCHWEIZERISCHEM RECHT, Zürich 1984, Vol. 1 at 306; Jaeger and Roelli, supra, n. 46 ad Art. 79/80 VVG.

9. Cf. BGE III 142.

10. Cf. BGE 81 III 143; Jaeger and Roelli, supra n. 13 et seq. Ad Art. 82, n. 53 et seq. ad Art. 79/80VVG; Wiret, supra at 216.

11. T. SPRECHER AND R. JETZER, EINFÜHRUNG IN DAS NEUE SCHULDBETREIBUNGS- UND KONKURSRECHT, Zürich 1997, at 62 et seq.; Fritzsche and Walder, supra at 549 et seq.

12. Cf. Art. 288a of the Swiss Dept Collection and Bankruptcy Act, FROIDEVAUX, LOI SUR LA POUR-SUITE DES DETTES ET LA FAILLITE, MODICATIONS AU 1ER JANVIER 1997, Bern 1997, at 227.

13. Cf. GAUGLER, DIE PAULIANISCHE ANFECHTUNG UNTER BESONDERER BERÜCKSICHTIGUNG DER LEBENSVERSICHERUNG, Vol. 2, Basel 1945, at 564; Amonn and Gasser, supra at 429.

14. Fritzsche and Walder, supra, Vol. 11 at 558 et seq.; Amonn and Gasser, supra at 431 et seq.; BGE 101 III 94; BGE 99 III 98.

15. H.Gaugler, supra at 542.

16. Fritzsche and Walder, supra. Vol.II at 561 et seq.; Amonn and Gasser, supra at 431 et seq.; cf. BGE 43 III 249; BGE 83 III 85.

17. BGE 79 III 99 et seq.; GULDENER, DAS INTERNATIONALE UND INTERKANTONALE ZIVIL-PROZESSRECHT DER SCHWEIZ, Zürich 1951, at 186.

18. Amonn and Gasser, supra at 407.

19. BGE 79 III 72.

20. Jaeger and Roelli, supra n. 78 ad Art. 79/80 VVG.

21. Berti, in KOMMENTAR ZUM SCHWEIZERISCHEN PRIVATRECHT, Basel 1996; Volken, IPRG Kommentar, Zürich 1993.

22. RYSER, DER VERSICHERUNGSVERTRAG IM INTERNATIONALEN PRIVATRECHT, Bern 1957, at 134; Jaeger and Roelli, n. 78 of Art. 79/80 VVG.

23. Cf. Berti, supra n. 11 ad Art. 171 IPRG.

24. Art. 81 Sect. 1 VVG.

25. Art. 81 Sect. 2 VVG.

Investing Offshore Through Portfolio Bonds

by Marc Sola,

How it works

The Portfolio Bond can be considered as a simple holding structure through which the investor (or his/her adviser) can direct the insurance company to invest in a wide range of investment vehicles such as stocks, bonds, mutual funds, or cash deposits. The underlying investments can be freely selected. Any investment can be held in the Portfolio Bond so long as the value can be established (e.g., non-listed stock, real estate and shares of the investor's own company).

Specifically, the investor closes a contract in his name with an insurance company, usually domiciled in an offshore tax haven. The insurance company opens an account with a bank selected by the investor, who in turn receives a policy from the insurance company. Legally, the investor is the client of the insurance company and the insurance company is a client of the bank. The investor can maintain full control of his assets as the policyowner or may choose to have the bank or an investment adviser manage the account. The policy value consists precisely of the value of the assets placed there by the insurance company on the investor's behalf and grows as managed. Legal entities and natural persons can be designated as beneficiaries. With certain annuities and insurance companies, the policyowner may be a legal entity. The person insured, however, must in all cases be a natural person.

Using Offshore Trusts, Annuities, and Portfolio Bonds

Overview of benefits

A Portfolio Bond provides the important benefits of an offshore account with a private bank: confidentiality and privacy, professional and individualized asset management, personal attention. As an insurance investment, a Portfolio Bond also provides the following substantial benefits:

> **Asset Protection.** Properly structured and established in the right jurisdiction, Portfolio Bonds enjoy legal protection from creditors. The laws applicable to asset protection with life insurance under Swiss law have been discussed by this author in detail in a previous issue of this Journal.[1] Interestingly, Liechtenstein's laws on the protection accorded life insurance policies and annuities is directly taken from the relevant Swiss laws.[2] To summarize, where a person not residing in Switzerland or Liechtenstein (the "policy owner") purchases an insurance policy from a Swiss or Liechtenstein insurance company and designates his spouse or his descendants as beneficiaries of such insurance policy, or irrevocably designates any other third party as beneficiary (e.g., a legal entity such as a Trust), this insurance policy will be protected by law against any debt collection procedures instituted by the creditors of the policy owner and will also not be included in any Swiss or Liechtenstein bankruptcy procedure in this regard. Even where a foreign judgment or court order expressly decrees the seizure of such policy, or its inclusion in the estate in bankruptcy, such an insurance policy may not be seized in Switzerland or Liechtenstein or included in the estate in bankruptcy, except where it is considered a fraudulent conveyance.[3]

In case of bankruptcy of the owner, protection is also guaranteed since the ownership is transferred to the beneficiaries automatically. Any instructions from the original policy owner which are forced upon him can no longer be acted upon; only his beneficiaries, as the new owners can give instructions to the insurance company.[4]

The Swiss insurance company can only act upon orders of the owner if his actions are deemed not to have been made under duress. If there is any evidence that an order has been forced upon the owner, such as in the case where the owner revokes in writing the beneficiary designation prior to a bankruptcy declaration, the insurance company cannot follow the instructions so issued. In such a case, it is important that the beneficiaries inform the insurance company.[5]

> **Separate and Simple Estate Planning Device.** Although a legal entity such as an estate planning trust can be named as irrevocable beneficiary of the Portfolio Bond, this type of investment is also well-suited for making distributions separate from the policyowner's estate. However, depending on his home jurisdiction, some compulsory portions for legal heirs may be reserved. Neither power-of-attorney, nor last will nor certificate of inheritance is required for payments to be made upon the owner's death. Beneficiaries get immediate access to the funds according to the payment method chosen by the policyowner.

Confidentiality and privacy. In addition to the confidentiality provided by a bank account in the name of the insurance company, a second layer of confidentiality is provided by insurance confidentiality. In certain jurisdictions insurance companies treat client information as would their banking counterparts. No information can be provided to any third party (natural person or legal entity). In Liechtenstein, for example, a separate insurance secrecy law protects the privacy of policyowners.[6] This law subjects not only persons affiliated with or acting on behalf of insurance undertakings to professional secrecy but also representatives of public agencies.[7]

With the introduction of U.S. withholding taxes on U.S. assets held in foreign accounts and with the tough reporting requirements for investments made through offshore trusts, offshore insurance vehicles, if correctly structured and from the right jurisdiction, can add strong privacy to your existing investments in a trust or a bank account.

Tax advantages. Unlike many offshore investments and structures, Portfolio Bonds are, in certain jurisdictions, completely free of local taxes. As far as income, capital gains, estate or withholding taxes are concerned, the law of the investor's tax domicile is decisive. In many countries insurance policies enjoy substantial tax benefits if correctly structured, i.e., the Portfolio Bond can be tailor-made to fit the legal requirements for privileged tax treatment. For U.S. persons this includes:

1. Tax deferral during the insured's life. The inside build-up of the Portfolio Bond is generally income and gains tax-free. For U.S. individuals and corporations with assets abroad, using a Portfolio Bond as a holding structure for these assets provides an efficient mechanism for sidestepping the new 31% withholding tax on income and gains from U.S. assets held in foreign accounts.
2. No income taxes on insurance proceeds. At the policyowner's death, the insurance proceeds are generally income tax exempt.
3. No estate taxes on insurance proceeds. With proper planning (such as through the use of an irrevocable trust under which the insured has no control or benefits) insurance proceeds can avoid estate taxation at the death of the insured.
4. No U.S. excise taxes under certain conditions. Unlike many other foreign insurance policies, Swiss policies are

not subject to the 1% U.S. excise tax on the purchase of foreign insurance and insurance premiums. This is a by-product of the adoption in 1998 of a revised Swiss-U.S. Double Tax Treaty and applies for premiums paid by a US citizen to an insurance company domiciled in Switzerland. Liechtenstein insurance companies are not "favored" by a similar tax treaty; Liechtenstein annuities are therefore subject to the excise tax. On the other hand, they are not subject to provisions with respect to disclosure of tax information, even where crimes have been committed under Liechtenstein law. The U.S. treaty with Switzerland, moreover, provides that the tax exemption applies "only to the extent that the risks covered by such premiums are not reinsured with a person not entitled to the benefits of this or any other Convention which provides exemption from these taxes."[8] The proof required to overcome this limitation — of whether the premiums are reinsured and, if so, whether the reinsurer is entitled to the exemption — could possibly defeat the privacy aspects of the policy, assuming the insurance companies would be willing to provide the information.

The Portfolio Bond qualifies as a life insurance policy for U.S. income tax purposes:

1. If it is based on a segregated investment account[9] and the segregated account is adequately diversified, i.e.:
   a) No more than 55% of the value of the total assets of the account is represented by any one investment;
   b) No more than 70% of the value of the total assets of the account is represented by any two investments;
   c) No more than 80% of the value of the total assets of the account is represented by any three investments; and
   d) No more than 90% of the value of the total assets of the account is represented by any four investments.[10] To

make certain that the segregated accounts comply with this "diversification rule", the portfolio needs to be rebalanced at the end of the first policy year and on a quarterly calendar basis thereafter.
2. If it satisfies Internal Revenue Code rules on death benefits.[11] These ensure that the insurance protection meets certain minimum requirements from the inception of the policy.[12]
3. If it is not self-directed, i.e., the policyowner must be deemed to have surrendered ownership or control of the assets. The income from Portfolio Bond is tax-free if the owner (or his adviser) is not managing the investments himself. Conversely, the insurance company is deemed to be the beneficial owner of the segregated account. Policyowners are permitted to choose investment categories, but they may not choose the actual investments. If they do, they are treated as the beneficial owners of the underlying assets, not the insurance company, and the income generated by those assets would be taxable.[13] Similarly, policyowners are not permitted to appoint an investment adviser to make the investment decisions on the underlying assets nor to control the adviser in such decisions.[14] The insurance company as beneficial owner is permitted to appoint and an independent investment adviser.

Trust compatibility. A Portfolio Bond is not necessarily a structure to replace offshore trusts, rather it can be used to complement a trust and to strengthen its protection. For example, assigning investments to an offshore trust is much cheaper and easier if they are grouped together under one Portfolio Bond. This greatly simplifies the tax treatment of the structure, and consequently, the reporting requirements, either through a reduction in the number of assets to be listed or through the fulfillment of the conditions for tax deferral.

Assets held within a portfolio bond are considered to be held by the insurance company. This allows an investor or a trust to hold assets privately also under the new regulations on U.S. withholding taxes on U.S. assets held in foreign accounts.

Insurance coverage. Depending on the investor's own needs and requirements for his heirs, additional insurance coverage can be provided in case of death. Coverage can also be adjusted during the term of the contract. This feature can be very important if a remaining spouse is forced to pay off a mortgage or if heirs need cash to buy out business partners.

Flexibility. Apart from being able to choose the amount of insurance coverage, the policyowner can choose to receive an annuity as well as choose to pay several premiums or a single one. As the underlying investments can be freely selected from a global palette of investments not available to the general public, the policy owner or his investment advisor (the latter for tax deferral) can optimize performance through wide diversification or hedging strategies.

Conclusion

Either in combination with offshore or domestic planning structures or alone, a Portfolio Bond is a useful and cost-effective tool to upgrade an existing portfolio of investments. A portfolio's features can be added or improved with regard to asset protection, confidentiality, reporting burden, insurance coverage, and flexibility, reducing costs and taxes, including transfer taxes as wealth passes from one generation to another. Whether they are concerned with taxes or the threat of litigation or are looking to diversify assets globally, with the Portfolio Bond, wealthy individuals can address those concerns as well as have access to leading investment managers and to investments otherwise not available to the public.

Endnotes

[1] Marc Sola, *Asset Protection through Swiss Life Insurance Policies,* ASSET PROTECTION JOURNAL, vol. 2, no. 1.

[2] Liechtenstein law on KONKURSPRIVILEG of June 1941 specifically adapts BUNDESGESETZ ÜBER DEN VERSICHERUNGSVERTRAG (the Swiss Federal Insurance Act or VVG) of April 1908.

[3] A policy will be considered a fraudulent conveyance within the meaning of Article 285 *et seq.* of the Swiss Debt Collection and Bankruptcy Act where the policy owner has designated the beneficiaries not more than one year before debt collection proceedings are initiated which eventually lead to a bankruptcy decree against the policy owner or to the seizure of the policy owner's assets. This condition will also be met where the beneficiary has been designated with the clear intent to damage creditors or to treat some creditors more favorably than others and the designation was made within five years from the date debt collection proceedings resulting in a bankruptcy decree or in the seizure of assets were initiated against the policy holder. The creditors concerned, however, need to prove not just the policy owner's intent but that the beneficiary had knowledge of the intent to defraud.

[4] Under Article 18 of the Swiss Code of Obligations, in case of discrepancy between the real intent and the intent expressed in writing, a person who receives such writing and knows that it does not express the real intent normally has to follow the real intent and ignore the writing.

[5] Article 81 Section 2 VVG.

[6] Article 44 VERSICHERUNGSAUFSICHTSGESETZ (VersAG).

[7] Article 44 Section 2 VersAG.
[8] 1998 U.S.-Switzerland Double Tax Treaty, Article 2, Paragraph 2, Subparagraph b.
[9] Internal Revenue Code, Section 817(h)(1)
[10] Treasury Regulations, Sections 1.817-5(b)(1) and 1.817-5(c)(1).
[11] The death benefits included in the policies do not make the annuities "debt instruments" — i.e., promises to pay a sum certain and, therefore, not tax deferred under Section 1275. They do not constitute debt instruments because they promise to pay a designated sum only if the owner dies. There is no guarantee of a particular sum if the owner cashes in the policy while he is alive.
[12] Alan R. Eber, *Creative Use of Foreign Entities for Asset Protection and Tax Planning: Part II*, ASSET PROTECTION JOURNAL, vol. 1, no. 2.
[13] Christoffersen v. United States, 749 F.2d 513 (8th Cir. 1984)
[14] IRC Section 817(h)(5).

www.ingramcontent.com/pod-product-compliance
Ingram Content Group UK Ltd.
Pitfield, Milton Keynes, MK11 3LW, UK
UKHW041428180426
11947UKWH00007B/346